THE PENINSULA
PORTRAIT OF A GRAND OLD LADY

PUBLISHED BY ROUNDHOUSE PUBLICATIONS (ASIA) LTD
409 YU YUET LAI BUILDING
43–55 WYNDHAM STREET
CENTRAL, HONG KONG

ISBN 962-7992-04-6
2ND PRINTING, 1997

PRINTED IN HONG KONG

FOREWORD:	JAN MORRIS
TEXT:	FRANCES BARTLETT
PHOTOGRAPHY:	LINCOLN POTTER
DESIGN:	GEORGE NGAN
EDITOR:	SALLY DE SOUZA
PHOTO EDITOR:	STEFAN CUCOS
DTP ARTWORK:	NEW STRATEGY LTD
INDEX:	FRANÇOISE PARKIN
PROJECT MANAGER:	DEBRA MAYNARD
COLOUR SEPARATION:	TWINSTAR GRAPHIC ART CO.
PRINTING:	PRINTING FORCE CO.

ALL PHOTOGRAPHY BY LINCOLN POTTER.
REMAINING PICTURES APPEAR COURTESY OF THE FOLLOWING: ALAN HO: 11, 46–7 (top),47 (bottom), 50, 52 (bottom), 53 (top and bottom), 54, 73, 83; THE HONGKONG AND SHANGHAI HOTELS, LIMITED: 44, 45, 46 (bottom left and right), 48 (top and bottom), 49, 50, 51, 52 (top left and right), 55, 56–7, 58 (bottom left), 59 (top and bottom), 60, 61 (top and bottom), 62, 63, 64, 65 (top and bottom), 66, 67, 68 (top and bottom), 69, 74, 75, 76, 79, 87, 90–1, 94, 95, 96, 97, 98, 99 (top and bottom), 101, 102 (bottom left and right), 104, 110, 112 (all), 113 (bottom), 116, 118, 119 (top and bottom), 121, 122, 123 (top and bottom), 124, 125, 126–7, 131, 133 (top and bottom), 136 (top), 139, 140, 143, 144, 145, 159 (top right), 161, 194, 198, 206, 216; HONG KONG GOVERNMENT PUBLIC RECORDS OFFICE: 115; THE HON. MICHAEL D. KADOORIE: 120; NEIL MCCALLUM: 157, 160; THE PENINSULA: 58 (top and right), 104 (top), 113 (top), 147, 154, 155, 158 (top and bottom), 159 (top left and bottom), 164, 165 (bottom), 168, 174, 186 (top and bottom), 187, 201, 202 (top and bottom); LOTHAR PRAGER: 87

Preceding pages, the Lobby in a tranquil moment; *right*, candelabra dating from the hotel's 1928 opening; *pages 6-7*, still life in antique silver bon-bon stand; *Contents pages*, frieze adorning the Lobby ceiling

CONT

ENTS

FOREWORD

There are many great and famous hotels in the world, but so far as I know only one is habitually known by its nickname. Mention 'The Pen' to world travellers in any continent, and they will know at once that you are talking about The Peninsula hotel, Kowloon, Hong Kong. What's more, their faces will almost certainly light up with recollected pleasure, because I have never met anyone who has not enjoyed a visit to this singularly happy institution.

For it *is* an institution – for 70 years one of the best-known in Hong Kong, a talisman of the place, in peace a prime centre of social life, in war taken over almost as a matter of course as a military headquarters, generals of all nations knowing which side their bread is buttered. Few people can now remember Hong Kong without The Pen, and few of us can imagine it, either. The Peninsula has changed down the years, as a successful hotel must – in the past decade it has astonishingly turned itself into a skyscraper: but its unique role in the life and reputation of the Territory has remained inviolate.

Most institutions are, of course, a little dull or stuffy. Many a celebrated hotel is regarded more with respect, even with awe, than with affection. The Pen is different. The Pen has always been fun, even when it has been entertaining the mighty of the world, and I think this is because of its origins. It began life as a very up-market transport hotel, serving both the railway passengers who came to Hong Kong by train across the Eurasian land mass, and the sea passengers who arrived by scheduled liner at the nearby quays of Kowloon. Later it also became a hub of Hong Kong's air travel,

with airline offices all around its Lobby, and merry air crews sometimes making exhibitions of themselves during off-duty hours.

It was, in short, a very luxurious caravanserai, enriched by all the variety, surprise and excitement of intercontinental travel, and this flavour of purposeful exuberance is its hallmark to this day. Gone are the airline counters and the devil-may-care pilots; few are the travellers who choose to come to Hong Kong via the Trans-Siberian Express; but The Peninsula still welcomes its guests with the particular blend of comfort, tolerance and amusement that wanderers always need, when they arrive from distant places and are hungry for indulgence.

And of course The Peninsula has all the indulgences one might expect of a crack cosmopolitan hotel at the end of the 20th century – all the videos and faxes and electric curtains and laser players, the magnificent cuisines, the foods flown in from Europe, the helipad, the Starck-designed brasserie, the fleet of Rolls-Royces, the glorious swimming pool. It is the flagship, as the times demand, of a glittering fleet of younger Peninsulas around the world.

But that is not the point of it. The point of it is this: that cherished down the decades by a loving dynasty of owners, The Pen has remained The Pen – not just one of the world's supreme hotels, but an institution so special that without a second thought, without gush or irony, we call it by its nickname.

Jan Morris

Left, the evocative harmony of old and new structures embodies The Pen's history of graceful evolution; *following pages*, standing tall and proud, The Pen again dominates the Kowloon peninsula

A DAY

IN THE Life

A DAY IN THE LIFE

A curious, repetitive beat echoes in the near-deserted Lobby. Two waiters, one on the west side, one on the east, are moving from chair to chair, slapping each seat, twice, with a rolled-up towel. It's 6 am, and not even the drumming of this brisk dusting dispels lingering echoes of the past. This is the room (though that seems far too modest a word for it; small wonder that "Lobby" has always merited being capitalised) that once inspired a disparate group of admirers to band together in a society dedicated to its preservation. This is where robber barons consorted with film stars; where refugees found shelter; where handshakes have launched a thousand deals; and where, only the day before, 1,200 scones were consumed at afternoon tea.

A day in the life of Hong Kong's Grand Old Lady resembles nothing so much as 24-hour theatre. There is, however, a slight shift in orientation: the curtain never comes down, for instance, and the players must not only know their lines, they must be talented improvisers. Nor are the footlights ever switched off – except when the bulbs need changing. And The Peninsula itself is more than a stage; it is the featured performer.

"I consider Hong Kong my second home." Glancing up at the exquisitely carved gilt that borders the recessed panels of the Lobby's neo-classical ceiling, Henry Rixon adds softly, "Right here." The Viennese-born American first came to Hong

Left, lobbying in The Peninsula; *below*, Chef Julien Bompard (*left*) and maître d' Rolf Heiniger (*third from right*) gather Gaddi's staff for a food-tasting

A morning view of the ever-changing face of Victoria Harbour is graced by enduring icons, the Star Ferry and the Clock Tower

Kong in 1959 when he was building his now sizeable import-export business. He tried one or two other hotels before registering at The Peninsula, "and once I stayed here, I never left." On his earliest visits, three or four a year sometimes, he and his suppliers discussed the supply and demand of Christmas decorations in the Lobby. He remembers meeting a local businessman who had a warehouse full of plastic flowers for sale. "He was just starting out, too"; Rixon pauses for dramatic effect before identifying the gentleman as Li Ka-Shing, sixth on *Forbes*' 1996 list of the world's richest men.

At this hour, even guests hurrying to make an early flight pause for a last look before moving toward the waiting Rolls-Royce. The massive pillars stand like sentinels, crowned with fierce gargoyles gazing silently, as they have done for nearly 70 years. The row of alcoves at mezzanine level and the empty orchestra bay, ornately defined with golden balustrades, resemble hushed theatre boxes. Through the tall, arched windows on the west side, the intersecting lines of the Cultural Centre sharpen in the deepening light, appearing like the outline of some motionless, futuristic barque.

Other than a soft murmur of conversation at Reception and the dissonant tune of cutlery being arranged in the wait station on the east side of the Lobby, The Pen's public face is peaceful. Behind the scenes, the heart of the hotel, known as "back-of-house", is beating faster in the prelude to Act One. In the kitchens, daybreak is signalled by fragrance rather than sunlight. A baker opens the door of a massive oven and removes a tray of lush, buttery croissants. He and a colleague have spent the night preparing 250 Danish pastries, 300 croissants, over 1,000 rolls and 120 muffins and setting the gleaming beaters of the Spiramatic to knead the dough for seven kinds of bread. The evocative scent of fresh baking wafts from the Pastry Kitchen, along the spotless corridors leading to the neighbouring kitchens, offices and dishwashing area.

For Lai Shui, on duty at the staff entrance, the busiest hour of his overnight shift is just beginning. Between now and 8 am, he will greet some 500 of The Peninsula's 800 staff as they pour into the hotel; room attendants, accountants, engineers, stewarding staff and waiters preparing for the day ahead. For 30 years, Lai Shui swung open The Peninsula's massive main doors, greeting guests with a wide smile. When a leg injury meant he was unable to spend all day on his feet, management created the possibility for him

A Lobby waiter is a blur of activity as he prepares for the breakfast hour

to continue his career with the hotel. Sitting comfortably at his post, Lai Shui invests his security function with a generous warmth that is appreciated by all staff. Occasionally, he is sought out by long-time guests who have missed his cheerful presence at the front door. They joke with him, call him "movie star", recalling his performance in the James Bond film, *The Man With the Golden Gun*, when the camera captured him welcoming Roger Moore to the hotel. "I had to open the door so many times," he chuckles. "The director kept calling 'cut'!"

The serenity of the Sun
Terrace invites all
manner of contemplation

Since 7.30 am, Receiving staff have been controlling the always imminent chaos of the loading area. Trucks roar in and before the wheels have come to a complete stop, men are jumping out of the cabs to shoulder crates of fresh Australian produce. Three to four times a week, The Peninsula takes delivery of 160 kg of Scottish salmon, 5 kg of Iranian caviar, 35 kg of Canadian bacon, 70 kg of spring chickens from France, 750 kg of salad, 3,000 oranges and 2,500 lemons from the United States. Today, Receiving staff await a call from the airport, alerting them to the arrival of the week's delivery of 70 kg of live fish and seafood from the Tung Sha Islands, off Taiwan, and destined for transfer to tanks in Spring Moon and the Chinese Kitchen.

Breakfast is the first act of the day. In the Verandah and the Lobby and on the Sun Terrace, waiters are feeding the computerised Micros order system with diners' requests for Birchermüesli, coddled eggs, spa-style omelettes and fresh fruit platters. On a Friday morning, few people have time for the Verandah's kippered

Scottish herring ("allow 15 minutes for preparation"). In the Lobby, conversation between regular guests and waiters, who greet each other by name, creates a muted hum. This is the Lobby's quietest meal hour, and one of the best times to appreciate its *cinquecento* splendour.

Poolside, a collection of umbrella-shaded tables is the preserve of those easing into the day in conditions of the utmost serenity. On the far side of the blue-tiled pool, water spouts from a lion's mouth and cascades in a soothing waterfall. Beyond the Sun Terrace lies an uninterrupted vista of Victoria Harbour and Hong Kong Island. The weather is clement, and the retractable glass screen which surrounds the entire area has been opened, and a faint breeze rustles the newspapers lying forgotten beside cups of steaming coffee; headlines cannot compete with the enthralling panorama. Time, technology and staggering reclamation efforts have altered the harbour, but it is still possible to envision the scene that inspired James Clavell's *Noble House* description: "There were hundreds of junks of every size and age – fishing vessels mostly – some powered, some ponderously sailing this way and that. Crammed double-decker ferries darted in and out of the traffic like so many dragonflies, and everywhere tiny sampans, oared or powered, scurried unafraid across the ordered sea-lanes." Contemporary diners watch tugboats towing lethargic dredgers and lighters laden with containers and imagine the view from latter-day colonial houses dappling the upper reaches of the Peak.

Below, morning ablutions for the Rolls-Royce fleet; *following pages*, guests stop by the Concierge desk for information and assistance, or sometimes just for a chat

Below the forecourt, the garage, which was added when the tower was built, is awash with water. The fleet of nine Silver Spur Rolls-Royces is given a bath each day at 8 am, and carefully polished on a weekly basis. A chauffeur is hard at work, buffing the immaculate bonnet of The Peninsula's pride and joy: a magnificent

Phantom II. Almost a contemporary of the hotel, the vehicle was first unveiled on the stand of Messrs. Barker & Co at the London Motor Show in October, 1934. Some 60 years later, it was restored by Ashton Keynes Vintage Restorations in England. Adapted for Hong Kong's climate and traffic conditions, the Phantom also has discreetly incorporated extras such as a telephone and a refrigerated drinks cabinet. The chauffeur glances at his watch. Soon it will be time to don his cap, place a picnic basket stuffed with luxurious goodies in the boot and draw up at the main doors to pick up the Argentinian couple who have requested a three-hour jaunt, circumnavigating Hong Kong Island.

Armed with room lists, keys and pagers, room attendants are fanning out to their allocated floors. "The guest in 1826 has a headache; I took her aspirins and tea an hour ago," advises one of the overnight shift attendants to her replacement (room attendants used to be called "room boys"; the introduction of women to the role necessitated a welcome change in vocabulary). Another attendant notes that he can expect to see familiar faces that afternoon: an American couple who don't choose to stay in a harbour-view room or a suite; they ask to be under Simon's care. He knows they will want extra pillows, a vase of fresh-cut flowers and the desk moved to face the window. The public area attendants move out, some to Chesa or Gaddi's, which can be cleaned thoroughly, and loudly, as these restaurants won't open until lunch time. Others begin conducting touch-ups of corridors, portions of the Lobby, the Verandah, Reception and other heavy-traffic areas.

Downstairs, the early morning hush is a memory and there's an air of lively anticipation. The sunlight blazes through the half-moon arches of the Lobby windows; voices rise to match and telephones seem to ring with greater urgency. The Concierge desk is a huddle of concentration and furrowed brows; Chief Concierge Christian Sussmann and his famously resourceful team will have to draw on a long sequence of contacts to fulfil a guest's request for a Vietnamese interpreter skilled in commercial translation. At the same time, there is the picnic by helicopter to see to and tickets for a supposedly sold-out musical to obtain.

All over The Peninsula, staff are preparing for the day ahead. "We have a corporate lunch for 40 in the Golden Pen, a pre-concert cocktail for 75 in the Salisbury Room, that's at 6.30 pm, and outside catering for Sir Run Run Shaw." Executive Manager in charge of Food & Beverage Jamal Hussain concludes his preview and Executive Housekeeper Ariane Iken reminds everyone that the end suites on floors 17 through 20 will be occupied by engineering staff installing the new telescopes. Sian Griffiths, Director of Public Relations, rhymes off the list of press who will be arriving in half an hour for the Gaddi's cooking class. "I'm taking a group of German travel agents on a tour at 3 pm," says Director of Marketing, Maria Sung. It will take her an hour to show off The Pen. Department heads attending the morning briefing in the General Manager's office have already discussed the arrivals list, noting VIPs and frequent guests, and General Manager Peter Borer and Resident Manager Ian Coughlan have indicated those they would like to greet personally.

General Manager Peter Borer: guiding The Peninsula into a new era

The atmosphere is brisk, efficient and friendly: like any hotel, The Peninsula thrives on team work, something her management corps has honed to perfection. Peter Borer describes himself as a conductor; "No one plays too loudly or out of tune or they answer to me – it's kind of a democratic dictatorship."

Putting down the telephone, an engineer moves to one of the hotel's two control stations. Housekeeping has relayed a guest's request for a little more coolness; the engineer will make the appropriate adjustment without having to enter the guest's room. Those members of the Engineering team's 38 staff who are on duty today check the schedule to see what alterations and repairs are to be handled. Throughout the day, the carpenters, painters, masons and air conditioning electricians and engineers may be called upon to take care of anything from a burned-out light bulb to replacing the software panel which drives the guest room technology.

"It took a lot of testing to find just the right blend of bitter and milk chocolate." Executive Chef Florian Trento is happy to explain how the Danish-made machine coats potato chips with chocolate, but declines to divulge the sinfully rich recipe. "Once we got the potato chips right, we started making chocolate-covered pretzels and popcorn." Gathering the flock of food writers assembled in the Banqueting Kitchen for the first-ever Gaddi's cooking class, he shepherds them on a tour of the rest of The Pen's western kitchens. In the VCR Kitchen (so-called because it serves the Verandah, Chesa and Room Service), cooks are scrambling eggs and folding wholewheat pancakes around mixtures of hot fruit. By contrast, Gaddi's Kitchen, next door, is a picture of calm as cooks quietly prepare stocks and sauces prior to

The first to meet and greet guests, the page boys are The Pen's ambassadors

the first day's orders. In the Room Service Kitchen, surrounded by stacks of wicker baskets, a bin of mangosteens and boxes of lychees, bananas, persimmon, star fruit and mangos, waiters quickly compose the 125 tasteful still lifes which will greet the day's new arrivals.

The doors of the Production Kitchen swing open and the tour group gasps as a heady brew of aromas assails their nostrils simultaneously. A tray of hams is being removed from the smoke oven, and in the far corner, a massive kettle simmers with gravy. "We go through 200 litres of gravy a day," says the chef. Smaller kettles hold 60-litre batches of fish, meat and vegetable stock. "This is The Peninsula's supermarket," he continues, aiming

the observers through the efficiently ordered rooms where fish and meat are chopped, filleted, smoked, portioned or minced, salads are made and dressings blended, vegetables are peeled and chopped, stocks and sauces are mixed.

Felix staff sit at the Long Table for a daily briefing in the Philippe Starck-designed brasserie

In the Pastry preparation area, a chef is carefully arranging trays of individually-wrapped cake slices destined for The Peninsula Boutique, while another is layering sponge cakes with generous dollops of cream. In the chill of the Chocolate Room are Cape gooseberries lightly dusted with sugar, chocolates filled with lychee, strawberry or banana cream and tiny, perfect fruit tarts.

"Most of the good restaurants in France are using Fleur de Sel; it's the top layer of sea salt produced by evaporation. Try some!" Gaddi's chef, Julien Bompard, proffers a plate of the snowy granules to the writers returned to him in the Banqueting Kitchen. Arranging the ingredients for Deep-Fried Ratatouille-Stuffed Mushrooms, he picks up a knife and starts peeling a mushroom. Class has begun.

The arcade shops are open for business. Some share a long history with The Peninsula. Eileen Kershaw's first boutique, set up in 1946, consisted of two guest rooms on the second floor. According to Mrs. Shia Ping Lee, who became Kershaw's partner in the 1950s, eventually taking over the concern, this informal shop catered mainly to Americans hungry for Chinese antiques. Now, the Eileen Kershaw boutique occupies the former Trans-World Airlines office. In the 1970s the airlines were encouraged to vacate the prime Lobby space they had been occupying, and Mrs. Lee took over the former check-in desks and installed the more salubrious names of Van Cleef & Arpels and Lalique. During the massive tower construction and renovation of the early 1990s, one shop at each end of the Lobby was restored to its original look (known as the "Davidoff style", as that is the only venue which had resisted alteration in recent decades) so that management could assess the effect. The response was overwhelming; "Davidoff-style" Lobby shopfronts were added to the contractors' list.

As noon approaches, the behind-the-scenes action builds to a controlled crescendo. A substantial portion of the more than 500 telephone calls handled daily by The Peninsula's operators are received around midday. Consulting the list of staff conversant with foreign languages, one operator advises a caller in slow but comprehensible German that she is putting him through to the more fluent Resident Manager. Punching numbers on their switchboards and calling up guest information on their computer terminals, the three women work efficiently, with no hint of pressure in their impossibly friendly voices.

The Peninsula serves an average of 3,000 meals daily; an exceptional number, considering that the largest function room holds just 120 people. Copper pots and frying

Friendly and unruffled, the voices of The Peninsula

pans sizzle and flash in the VCR and Gaddi's kitchens as first orders pop out of the Micros computer terminal. A section cook places a mini window box of fresh herbs on a shelf and arranges a row of heavy silver gravy boats. In the Cold Kitchen, a cook meticulously prepares pâté appetisers. Waiters in Gaddi's and the Verandah begin to seat the early diners, greeting most of them by name.

As lunchtime approaches, the behind-the-scenes pace builds

Cleavers flash in the lower level of the Chinese Kitchen as cooks deftly slice meat, peel garlic bulbs and chop pickled mustard greens. An apprentice peels asparagus amid a mounting pile of fragrant, shredded greenery, tossing the denuded stalks into a plastic container. On the wok range, bunches of *choy sum* soak in running water. There's little talk: the cacophony of air conditioners and flaming woks precludes easy conversation. A cook measures amounts of sugar and chicken stock powder on a Chinese weigh scale. He expertly nudges the heat control lever with his knee and the flame – and the decibel level – rises. The stove-top temperature can reach 200° celsius almost instantly, ideal for the quick-frying techniques favoured in Cantonese cooking. Heating a blend of soy and chilli sauces and chicken stock in a wok, the

cook pours it into a pot and puts it to one side, then he pours water into the wok, stirs vigorously with a bamboo whisk and empties the liquid into a drain running along the edge of the range.

Upstairs, orders are popping out of the Micros terminal. Three cooks have been making *dim sum* here since 8 am; steaming glutinous rice to wrap in lotus leaves, mixing and shaping shark's fin *siu mai*, topped with a pert glaze of glass noodles, enfolding shrimps or sweet barbecued pork in rich dumpling pastry. In the Barbecue Room, a large fan is trained on a row of ducks and pigeons for at least an hour before they're hung on hooks inside the barrel-shaped oven. The barbecue cook removes baked strips of honeyed pork and places them alongside ducks and quail which have already seen the inside of the oven. In the main kitchen area, one cook prepares the orders, while the other two continue making fresh dumplings. He stacks baskets of *dim sum* to skyscraper heights on the massive steamer and clips the printed order to the lid with an incongruous, yet utilitarian plastic clothespin.

The second act is well underway. Waiters, cooks, mâitre d's, stewarding staff and customers play their roles in the dining hour drama, from the elegant chic of the Verandah to the impeccably synchronised flourish of silver covers lifting off in Gaddi's, from the public whirl of the Lobby to the snug warmth of Chesa.

In the Main Service Bar, the senior barman is replenishing stocks in the climate-controlled storeroom. Ten years ago, the labels would have indicated mainly French vintages, supplemented by limited German stocks. While both countries are still very well represented, The Peninsula's geographic coverage has extended to

include a rich variety of New World wines. Alongside prized bottles of Château Petrus and Château Lynch-Bages can be found Australian chardonnay and Sonoma cabernet sauvignon. The hotel's wine cellar is the most extensive in Asia, with a general list of more than 400 wines, of which there are often two or three vintages of one wine, as well as a Rare Vintage List. The one-page Private Wine List records the holdings of a small coterie of frequent guests and connoisseurs for whom the Beverage Manager obtains personal supplies, which are then stored in the hotel.

Gaining possession of a mid-afternoon table in the Lobby takes patience. During the wait, tastebuds tend to become agitated at the sight of freshly-baked scones being lavishly spread with Devonshire clotted cream or strawberry preserves and crumpets dripping with New Zealand honey. Staff somehow keep track of who is to be seated next, creating order out of what management has dubbed "the war zone": afternoon tea. Fortunately, the usual rush hour at Reception has subsided by 2.30 pm, and baggage attendants with their padded luggage carts need cut only a few disruptive swathes through the crowds.

Far left and left, cooking with a French flourish in Gaddi's Kitchen; *below,* temperatures rise in the Spring Moon Kitchen

A waiter encountering a cluster of shoppers blocking his route from kitchen to table barely blinks as he moves around them with an almost balletic step; he and his colleagues have a finely tuned sixth sense that allows them to navigate meandering passers-by while balancing with one hand a silver tray which weighs eight pounds *before* it is piled high with a three-tier cake tray,

Preceding pages, afternoon tea in the Lobby, where "what attracts the clientele is the clientele"; *above,* waiters await their orders

chinaware and heavy silver pots of tea and coffee. A few tourists glance up from their maps, as entertained by this improvised dance as by the sightseeing campaign they are planning. Business people and groups of shoppers, accustomed to the hustle, discuss trends and deals over a double espresso. Bursts of laughter punctuate the dull roar of conversation vying with The Lobby Strings' classical repertoire.

Picking up an aged Roberts & Belk silver milk jug, a Stewarding officer seated in a peaceful corner back-of-house dabs a little polish on a cloth and removes the tiniest discoloration from around the jug's handle. Some 80 per cent of The Peninsula's silver dates from 1928 and much of it is still in daily use. The fancy bon-bon dishes grace buffet tables, decorated with truffles and chocolates, while the ornate cake stands, three to four feet in diameter, lend an old-world grace to weddings and anniversaries. In the Silver Store are oyster forks, snail forks, dessert forks, two types of fish fork, meat forks and serving forks. There are Davidoff cigar-cutters, lobster picks, asparagus tongs and butter dishes with strainers (one of the few items to have been retired in recent years, along with the jam pot holders). Candlesticks, punch bowls and grated cheese dishes, cocktail strainers, lemon squeezers, cocktail mixing spoons and soda spoons are meticulously catalogued and stored in the climate-controlled room.

"Day and night we are polishing silver," says David Kwok, Chief Steward. Every morning, six to eight Stewarding staff join in a polishing session; every afternoon three or four people apply environmentally-friendly cleansing powder to a continual stream of trays, jugs, plates and pots which are in daily use throughout the hotel. Milk jugs, tea and coffee pots are shipped to England on a regular basis for re-silvering. Larger pieces, like the roast beef stand which stood in the original Main Banqueting Hall, are touched up every five or so years. A 1989 assessment put a valuation of HK$5 million on the whole collection; HK$350,000 is spent each year on repair and replacement.

Late afternoon, in the calm before the evening flurry of activity, is when chefs meet with the Food & Beverage cost controller to discuss menu pricing. Housekeeping and Food & Beverage staff drop into the Purchasing department. Responsible for sourcing and negotiating with suppliers of new items, the Purchasing staff patiently deal with one urgent request after another.

Surrounded by silver both contemporary and antique, Stewarding staff conduct a daily polishing session

By 5 pm, back-of-house is warming up for the evening show. The Linen Room staff have completed the meticulous guest room linen exchange. It would be impossible for them to count every one of the approximately 5,000 guest room towels, sheets and duvet covers that are sorted and sent for cleaning every afternoon. Instead, they conduct spot checks, cross-checking against the lists prepared by Housekeeping. That morning, between 6,000 and 7,000 restaurant napkins and tablecloths were exchanged by Food & Beverage staff.

Right and below, precision and creativity combine to beautiful effect, ensuring an unforgettable wedding reception in the Salisbury Room

Flower Room experts are putting the finishing touches on the elaborate Salisbury Room arrangements. They have worked closely with the client, who requested specific colours to represent the guest of honour's origins. Soon, the evening florist will be sorting and storing the daily delivery of blooms from Holland. Day-shift room attendants are briefing their successors. A host of restaurant staff and cooks who will be working that evening are choosing a meal from the three menus on offer at Chui Dim, the staff restaurant.

—◆◆◆—

A frisson of anticipation signals the commencement of the evening act. "It's show time!" says Jamal Hussain at 5.30 pm, as he starts his hour-long restaurant rounds. At each stop, he has a quick word with the manager, scans the bookings and walks through the venue, making sure that all is in perfect order. The evening room attendants are turning down beds, freshening towels, touching up fruit baskets, straightening clothing and refilling the ice bucket. "Where should I eat tonight?

I haven't made a booking yet," asks one guest. The attendant recommends Felix and offers to telephone the restaurant. "Where can we eat *dim sum*?" The young couple on their first visit to Hong Kong want their first meal to be authentic Chinese. Their room attendant explains that *dim sum* is usually enjoyed at breakfast or lunch. "But Room Service will prepare some for you, or you could try other Cantonese dishes at Spring Moon."

Evenings, The Peninsula preens shamelessly, showing off her flair for the traditional and the contemporary. On the first floor, the 70-year-old French chandeliers in Gaddi's cast a brilliantine glow and the dark-panelled homeliness of Chesa offers a warm embrace. Some 27 floors above, Felix, the brainchild of eccentric French

Setting the scene in Felix's private room

designer Philippe Starck, is a stunning blend of dark mahogany and aluminium reliefs. And on the 30th floor, the singular China Clipper helipad lounge combines sophisticated air travel technology with a passionate tribute to the early pioneers of aviation.

In the same moment, a group of twenty-something Cantonese movie stars will take over Felix's illuminated dance floor; Rolf Heiniger will create a Caesar Salad for a long-time Gaddi's patron while his waiters croon "Happy Birthday" to a budding tycoon celebrating with his friends; there will be a post-concert rush for cocktails, coffee and dessert in the Lobby; old friends will linger over a glass of 1953 armagnac in Chesa; the pianist in the Bar will sing a Nat King Cole song upon request; a family reunion in the Verandah will end with laughter and reminiscence; half-empty cognac bottles will dot the table of a successful corporate dinner being held in Spring Moon.

Later, The Grand Old Lady is peaceful, but she is anything but asleep. Behind the Reception desk, the night auditors are beginning to wade through the day's receipts from Front Office cashiers and Food & Beverage wait staff. By dawn, they will have finished a complete reconciliation, posted the room revenues and produced another daily revenue report. At 2 am, a public area attendant with a portable vacuum cleaner strapped to his back investigates the nooks and crannies under Lobby tables and around pillars. There's a low buzz as an electric hoist raises a window cleaner to the uppermost reaches of the arched windows. High heels click on the marble floor and quiet giggles echo briefly as a quartet of wedding guests, one burgundy-gowned woman casually holding the bride's bouquet, its blue satin ribbons trailing to the ground, emerge from the lifts and, yawning, make their way toward the front door and a waiting taxi.

Right, night throws a dramatic aspect on the contrasting façades

After a brief intermission, one of Hong Kong's longest running shows will start again.

The INSPI

THE INSPIRATION

When The Peninsula hotel first welcomed the public, on December 11, 1928, it was already a survivor. As that morning's comparatively subdued function for select luminaries in the civil service and military and business worlds gave way to the long-awaited and more boisterous Open House at noon, as the crowds marvelled at the 7,500-square-foot *cinquecento* Lobby — so described because the classical design recalled the style which predominated in 16th-century Italy — at its soaring marble pillars and elaborate chandeliers, at the perfect staircase which inspired grand entrances from beautifully coiffed and coutured women, at the incredible variety of dining and imbibing possibilities

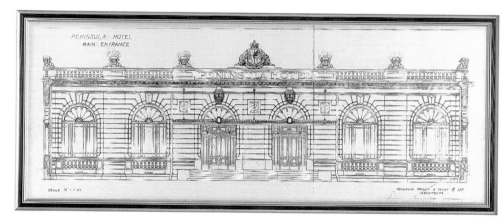

afforded by the Moorish Bar, the domed Main Banqueting Hall, the Children's Dining Room, the Tea Lounge, the Roof Garden and the Rose Room, and as furiously scribbling newspaper reporters summoned up every adjective in their repertoire in an effort to convey the splendour, the directors of The Hongkong and Shanghai Hotels, Limited no doubt felt a special sense of triumph as they reflected on the years they had spent coaxing into being the "finest hotel east of Suez".

Preceding pages, nymphs, creatures and delicate patterns on the Lobby ceiling were created by master craftsmen from Shanghai; *left, and above,* architect's drawings of the façade and main entrance

Among the officials was a young Lawrence (later Lord) and Horace (later Sir Horace) Kadoorie, representing their father Sir Elly, who had become a director of The Hongkong and Shanghai Hotels, Limited that year. "We were suitably attired in morning coats," Sir Horace recalled in his address to a similarly celebratory crowd 50 years on. "We must have been of a hardier generation then as we awaited His

Above, centre of commerce and society, Hong Kong Island overshadowed Kowloon until the 1930s; *below left, and right,* The Peak Hotel was the second in the company's portfolio

Excellency the Acting Governor's arrival with the overhead fans stirring the turbid and stifling atmosphere!" The blazing heat was recalled by Lord Kadoorie over 60 years later: "It was a very hot day, and it was a great day, because Jimmy Taggart, whose idea it was to build a Peninsula, had been laughed at. They said he'd constructed a white elephant on the Kowloon side and that nobody would ever live there." The brothers' attendance at the ground-breaking ceremony early in the decade had marked their first official involvement with the hotel which was to become woven into the fabric of their lives.

Six storeys high, the light grey Renaissance-style building easily dominated the landscape. Just as it had already dominated newspaper banners and countless corporate discussions for more years than its founders cared to remember, and just as it was soon to dominate an extravagantly hectic social life. Yet, somehow, rather than dwarfing its sleepy surroundings on Kowloon peninsula, the towering presence redefining the skyline seemed instead to lend its environment an air of richness, majesty even. Its very existence spoke of an immutable optimism.

As the Governor pointed out that day in 1928, Taggart's was the "inspiring mind" behind The Peninsula. The Scottish manager of The Hongkong Hotel had been promoted to managing director of The Hongkong Hotels Limited in 1922. Already a venerable institution in the young

colony, it was the first hotel company in the Far East: incorporated in 1866 it was one of the first companies in the Territory to be granted a listing on the Hong Kong stock exchange. Taggart's new role almost coincided with the company's acquisition of The Shanghai Hotels Limited, and its properties in Shanghai (The Astor House and The Palace Hotel; the Majestic Hotel was purchased in 1924) and Beijing (The Grand Hotel des Wagon-Lits). To reflect the broader range of operation, it was renamed The Hongkong and Shanghai Hotels, Limited. The company's expansion

The Ballroom of The Repulse Bay Hotel

plans were ambitious and Taggart's proposal to build a world-famous hotel, offering luxury and services never before available in the Far East, fell on fertile ground. Innumerable setbacks would eventually turn certain of the formerly supportive board members into angry challengers. "It is three years since we had a return on capital," complained one, "this after having paid dividends without a break for 24 years." Fortunately, Taggart was gifted not only with vision, but the force to carry it through.

Even the strongest of wills behind The Peninsula's creation had been sorely tried by the vexing complications of a troubled political and economic scene that conspired to delay, and indeed threaten, its opening. Work was begun on January 2, 1922, but was abruptly halted when the original plans were deemed unsuitable. A new scheme was drawn up and piling commenced. The company's

annual report for the year announced the completion date had changed from 1924 to 1926, explaining that: "…it was necessary to sink some 600 piles and, as is inevitable with foundation work, a considerable period had to elapse during which there was little to show."

By 1925, when the building was already the highest in Kowloon, the opening was again delayed. A special board meeting was convened to discuss cancelling the project entirely, but the board finally concluded that "it is impossible to stop The Peninsula work now in progress without most seriously damaging the interests of the company and placing its credit in jeopardy". Board members had to steel their determination still further when a General Strike began on June 30, 1925, and paralysed Hong Kong for four months. Worse was yet to come.

Hong Kong was perennially lacking in accommodation. Since the Union Jack had been planted on Possession Point in 1841, the Territory had prospered. For decades, the British had chaffed at the restrictions imposed on them by the Chinese which limited their access to the mainland in Canton (Guangzhou), which forbade them carrying arms while in that city and prevented them from learning the Chinese language. For its part, the Chinese government's objections to Britain's mammoth trade in opium grew considerably more vociferous. The conflict that was unleashed by China's efforts to eradicate the opium trade gave the Chief Superintendent of Trade, Captain Charles Elliot, R.N., the opening he needed to send in the gunboats and demand title to the island of Hong Kong.

In London, a displeased Lord Palmerston, who had hoped his side would gain a larger, if not more recognisable, chunk of China, launched his famous "barren rock" opinion of the acquisition. Despite the

Queen's Road in Central

British government's lack of appreciation, traders and merchants quickly took advantage of the secure, protected harbour, seeing the potential in the opening up of trading rights with China. By the time Hong Kong formally became a British possession on June 26, 1843, an enterprising frontier town had erupted into existence.

Hong Kong Island grew quickly to become the Territory's centre of commerce. Kowloon, a later addition, was regarded with the disdain usually afforded younger siblings, and was generally considered a backwater. The southern tip of the Kowloon peninsula had been acquired in 1860, in The Convention of Peking, which ended the second Anglo-Chinese War. The British enlarged their territory still further in

1898 with the 99-year lease of the rest of the peninsula and its immediate environs, along with the islands of the archipelago surrounding Hong Kong.

Hong Kong's notorious energy was apparent right from the start. What had been a sleepy scattering of Chinese fishing villages rapidly metamorphosed into a noisily thriving port town. The land of opportunity attracted merchants, entrepreneurs, financiers, civil servants, soldiers of all nationalities. The British were there in numbers, of course, but also Indians, Americans, Scots, Portuguese, Armenians and Chinese.

Among the shareholders, directors and visionaries of The Hongkong and Shanghai Hotels, Limited were some of the Territory's most innovative entrepreneurs. Men such as Sir Paul Chater, the wealthy Calcutta-born merchant, and Sir Robert Ho-Tung, comprador of Jardine, Matheson, and prominent in Chinese business and charitable circles. Also playing an integral role was Sir Ellis Kadoorie, who forged a rare reputation for combining business acumen with philanthropy and who was to lay the foundations of a family dynasty which would be central to The Peninsula's prominence and its fortunes.

Photo of Nathan Road, taken by a soldier of the 2nd Battalion Scots Guards, 1927

To early 20th-century Hong Kong's elaborately ordered society (and well into the mid-1900s), Kowloon was a faintly amusing location; one which smacked of both the rural and the risqué. "Are you married, or do you live in Kowloon?" quizzed society matrons of newcomers, the inference being that anyone who lived across the harbour must be embroiled in an inter-racial relationship and well beyond the pale in social terms. Other salacious reasons for a Kowloon address were generally held to be connected with debts and/or scandal, which lent a delicious irony to the alacrity with which The Peninsula hotel ascended the Territory's well-structured social ladder. Kowloon, in fact, had much to recommend it.

Sir Robert Ho-Tung, comprador and philanthropist, was on the board of The Hongkong and Shanghai Hotels, Limited

Flat terrain, wide, well-planned streets lined with trees and orderly rows of two- and three-storey mainly residential buildings gave it a less jumbled look than its hilly neighbour across the water. True, it could claim few grand structures; Tsim Sha Tsui then was notable only for the military barracks, the dockyards, the Star Ferry and, since 1910, the Kowloon-Canton Railway Station. Hong Kong Island residents may not have given the peninsula a glance, but ship's captains set their chronometers by the dropping of an enormous copper ball suspended from the top of the Royal Observatory tower on Kowloon every day at 1 pm. Radio time signals, introduced in 1935, brought the copper ball to a halt.

It was the railway station, with its steam engines connecting Hong Kong to Europe via Beijing or Moscow, which ultimately made Site 1461, virtually on the tip of the peninsula and across from the train station, an ideal location for a grand railway hotel. Throughout the early 1920s, Hong Kongers could see, across the harbour bustling with Chinese junks, traders' ships, military vessels and freighters, the gradual rise of The Peninsula, its façade shrouded in bamboo scaffolding.

FOUNDATIONS OF A DYNASTY

Right, Sir Elly Kadoorie, with sons Lawrence and Horace; *below,* Sir Ellis Kadoorie; *bottom,* the Bund in Shanghai

During the 1880s, two scions of a wealthy Baghdad family of merchants travelled East. The elder brother settled in Hong Kong; the younger in Shanghai. Together, they made the Kadoorie name synonymous as much for their generosity toward those less fortunate as for the riches they accumulated.

Elly Kadoorie came to Shanghai in 1880 and joined the first Iraqi Jewish firm in the city, David Sassoon & Sons. He soon struck out on his own and became a successful merchant banker, owner of real-estate and hotels and rubber plantations. Elly's elder brother, Ellis, was just 18 when he arrived in Hong Kong in 1883. He first set up as a broker, then a merchant and a financier, proving exceedingly successful in all his ventures, and eventually acquired control of the China Light & Power Company, Limited. In 1906, Ellis set in motion an involvement which would occupy not only his brother, but succeeding generations of Kadoories. He purchased a major holding of some 20,000 shares in The Hongkong Hotels Limited, and in 1914 was invited to take a seat on the company's board.

The Kadoorie brothers' reputation for and attitude towards public benefaction, coupled with their innate warmth and graciousness, won them a special place in people's hearts. Elly Kadoorie had commented that his own experiences with poverty had led him to a firm belief that

"wealth is a sacred trust to be administered for the good of society". Ellis funded Ellis Kadoorie schools and hospitals in Iraq, China and Hong Kong, and was instrumental in establishing Hong Kong's Helena May Institute. He contributed towards a new school for the colony's Indian children and endowed scholarships for underprivileged Indian children. He assisted the building fund for a European YMCA. And when World War I broke out, he spearheaded support for a War Fund appeal to buy war planes.

When in 1917 Ellis was dubbed Sir Ellis Kadoorie, Order of the Knights Bachelor, the *South China Morning Post* paid him warm tribute. "It is pleasing indeed, to see that recognition of his benefactions has come – and all the more pleasing to his many friends for the reason that Sir Ellis Kadoorie's generous courteous nature has made him well liked by all." During his eight-year term, The Hongkong Hotels Limited made great strides towards becoming a major Far East hotel chain. In 1922, upon the company's acquisition of an 85 per cent controlling interest in The Shanghai Hotels Limited, which owned The Astor House and The Palace Hotel in Shanghai and approximately 60 per cent of the Grand Hotel des Wagons-Lits in Peking, its name was changed to The Hongkong and Shanghai Hotels, Limited.

The Astor House, in the American Settlement, which later became part of the International Settlement, was the largest of

the Shanghai hotels. The Palace Hotel, at the corner of the city's main thoroughfare, Nanking Road, is today part of The Peace Hotel on the Bund. The Majestic Hotel was part of the portfolio for only six years, from 1924 to 1930. As Harriet Sergeant describes in *Shanghai: Collision Point of Cultures*, it had originally been a private house for a Captain McBain who had resisted strong social pressure to marry the daughter of a sampan

Above, exterior of the Astor Hotel in Shanghai; *below*, the hotel's dining room

Main Dining Room, Astor House, Shanghai, China.

Palace Hotel S'hai

woman who cleaned his ship. The future Majestic Hotel was built for the couple and their family of nine children.

Sadly, Sir Ellis was never to see The Peninsula project even approach its completion. On February 24, 1922, he succumbed to a heart attack at the age of 57. Under the headline, "A Loveable Man and a Generous Benefactor", the *South China Morning Post* spoke for countless members of the community when it wrote: "…in every quarter there was the sincerest expression of regret, coupled with genuine appreciation of Sir Ellis for his unassuming personal qualities, his ability, and for his generous benefactions and hospitality. Few of the community have not enjoyed at one time or another his kindly thought. … In Hong Kong, Shanghai, Canton and elsewhere, he was held in high respect and more. For those quiet qualities one looks for so often in vain in the Far East, he was well liked."

Sir Elly (he had been knighted in 1926) was invited to become a member of The Hongkong and Shanghai Hotels, Limited board in 1928. With his brother, he was an early supporter of The Peninsula project. They, of all people, could be described as having a truly visionary quality and their years conducting business in Hong Kong had instilled strong confidence in a city which had achieved so much in such a short period. Mavericks of their time, the Kadoorie brothers were not ones to shy away from a risk. The Peninsula would prove their instincts faultless, yet again.

With Sir Elly on the board, the way was paved for his sons, Lawrence and Horace, to carve out roles for themselves in the hotel company. On April 15, 1937, Sir Elly resigned his seat and Lawrence was transferred from Shanghai to take his father's place. He was immediately appointed Chairman, a role which was later assumed by Horace, in 1946.

In February, 1927, the scaffolding was at last dismantled and The Peninsula did indeed open its doors, but instead of the anticipated passengers of luxury ocean-liners, in marched the 2nd Battalion Coldstream Guards and a battalion of the Devonshire Regiment. Britain had viewed with trepidation the civil wars dividing the mainland in the mid-1920s and the anti-foreign and anti-British boycott imposed by Chiang Kai-shek and his Kuomintang forces. The effects of the civil unrest had already manifested themselves in the Territory with the General Strike of 1925 which had brought the city to a standstill for four months. Concerned for its business interests and citizens in Shanghai, Britain rushed troops to Hong Kong for possible military action against the Kuomintang. Now that The Peninsula's structural work was complete, the Military Authorities saw it as an ideal location for a temporary barracks.

Despite their consternation, the Company's board members naturally gave the military their full support and for the next 14 months the uncarpeted halls of The Peninsula echoed with the thud of heavy boots and troops drilled every morning on Nathan Road, bayonets at the ready. When the soldiers eventually moved out, never having been sent to Shanghai after all, repair teams moved in to replace the flooring and all the bathtubs, which, judging by the damage, they speculated must have served as storage places for rifles and bayonets.

Above, the first "guests" to check in to The Peninsula were British soldiers; *following pages*, front elevation, April 1927

Almost two years later, James Taggart referred to these first "guests" in his address to the Acting Governor, the Hon. W.T. Southorn, saying: "The Peninsula has, during the period of its construction, experienced a somewhat chequered career in that much has happened to delay its progress towards the realisation of the hopes of those responsible for its inception, its erection and the ceremony which Your

Above and right, opening day at last! Society turned out in force on December 11, 1928, to tour the magnificent hotel; *below*, a newspaper advertisement detailed the musical programme

Excellency is so kindly performing. I would like to mention here that the last incident in the foregoing relation is one upon which we look back with feelings of pride. I refer to the many months in which we had the honour of housing a large portion of H.M. Forces…" No doubt the crowd suspected a certain amount of tongue-in-cheek in Taggart's tactful speech.

"I was present at the opening ceremony – as a nine-year-old," recounted T.I. Hall, six decades on. "That day, my principal anxiety was to escape 'a fate worse than death itself' should I not conduct myself in a manner befitting the occasion; I cannot recall any particular misdemeanour." Another young lad was similarly relieved that the day went smoothly. Just as he had been coached for the past month, Chan Pak, a 12-year-old page boy, wearing a costume he described as that of a "charming prince", walked up to the Acting Governor's wife and, with a graceful bow, shyly presented her with

a large bouquet of gold and bronze chrysanthemums. He little dreamed that some 66 years later, after nearly a lifetime with The Peninsula, he would perform the same task at another grand opening.

All that day and well into the evening, a steady stream of elegantly dressed men and women travelled across the Fragrant Harbour by Star Ferry, junk or sampan, travelling the last few hundred feet by rickshaw or on beautifully-shod foot. In the forecourt, the fragrance of lingering perfume blended with the sultry sea breeze and the sounds of music and laughter poured from windows ablaze with light. Doormen clad in neat black

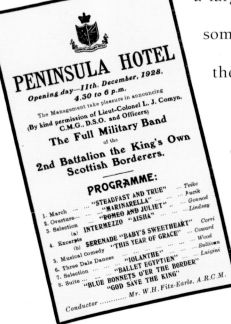

PENINSULA HOTEL

Opening day—11th. December, 1928.
4.30 to 6 p.m.

The Management take pleasure in announcing
(By kind permission of Lieut-Colonel L. J. Comyn,
C.M.G., D.S.O. and Officers)

The Full Military Band
of the
2nd Battalion the King's Own
Scottish Borderers.

PROGRAMME:

1. March .... "STEADFAST AND TRUE" ... *Teike*
2. Overture .... "MARINARELLA" .... *Fucik*
3. Selection .... "ROMEO AND JULIET" ..... *Gounod*
   (a) INTERMEZZO "AISHA" .... *Lindsay*
4. Excerpts SERENADE "BABY'S SWEETHEART" ... *Corri*
   (b) Musical Comedy "THIS YEAR OF GRACE" .. *Coward*
5. Three Dale Dances .... *Wood*
6. Selection .... "IOLANTHE" .... *Sullivan*
7. Selection ..... "BALLET EGYPTIEN" .... *Luigini*
8. Suite ... "BLUE BONNETS O'ER THE BORDER"
             "GOD SAVE THE KING"

Conductor .... Mr. W.H. Fitz-Earle, A.R.C.M.

uniforms and distinctive "pillbox" hats opened the great doors with a flourish, welcoming

Hong Kong to the greatest party of the decade. Folk sipped tea under the sky-blue

dome of the Main Banqueting Hall; danced to live music among the Doric columns

of the Roof Garden; enjoyed cocktails in the Moorish Bar. Gentlemen tried out the

seats in the Barber Shop and decided a trim was in order. The band of the King's

Own Scottish Borderers entertained on the first floor Terrace. The crowds explored

every nook and cranny. "All is magnificent, well-appointed," one newspaper would

report. An American woman put it more informally: "It makes me feel like a million

dollars. I'd feel rich here even if I hadn't a dime in my bag."

The festivities culminated in a Carnival Dinner Dance, with

guests decked out in Fancy or Evening Dress, in the Roof Garden

Ballroom. Tickets cost just HK$4 per person, including dinner. The Peninsula,

glittering and triumphant, filled the front pages of the *South China Morning*

Post, the *Hongkong Telegraph* and the *Hong Kong Daily News*: "Opening of

Peninsula Hotel – Finest Hotel in the Far East"; "The Courage and

Foresight of our Predecessors".

THE FINEST HOTEL EAST OF SUEZ

The design and construction of The Peninsula was entrusted to Hong Kong Realty & Trust Co. Ltd., Civil Engineers and Architects. The hotel's exterior, a textured grey-

The Ballroom was destined to become the heart of the society swirl

green plaster over brick on a reinforced concrete structure, adorned with dignified flourishes and cornices created by renowned Shanghai craftsmen, was often described as 'sombre' in those early years. No such restraint – in description or reality – characterised the interior.

In the frenzied months leading up to the grand opening, an army of repairmen laboured to remove all traces of the army of soldiers who had just quit the hotel. At the same time, hundreds of carpenters, plasterers, metalworkers, stained-glass artists and painters, also from Shanghai, carried out the long-interrupted task of finishing ceilings, walls, stairs, windows and doors. Between them, the architects, designers and craftsmen, working in concert with dedicated hotelier James Taggart, created a building of breathtaking grandeur. If the splendour gave the first overwhelming impression, the impeccable attention to infinite detail communicated a lasting sensation of superb taste and quality.

It began in the Lobby, where tall pillars met the ceiling's mirror-work cherubs with a flourish of classical mouldings. The rotating blades of long ceiling fans caused the ornate Viennese chandeliers to sway ever so slightly. The main staircase was created for grand entrances, its balustrade wound around with sinuous curlicues. The floor was of imported decorative tiles.

Above the Lobby, the Tea Lounge featured elaborate plaster work: bows, swags, garlands and medallions covered the walls, pillars and beams. The floor was covered with a plush red carpet. On the first floor of the West Wing was a Queen Anne-style Reading Room, Children's Dining Room and accompanying lounge decorated

like a nursery with characters from fairy tales and nursery rhymes.

Guest rooms were lit by beautifully carved

wooden chandeliers made in Shanghai. Much of the furniture was also made in that city, which was acknowledged as having superior craftsmen to Hong Kong. Amazingly, all the rooms – including corridors and public areas – were fitted with radiators.

From the time The Peninsula was conceived, The Hongkong and Shanghai Hotels, Limited had been determined to present, as James Taggart put it on opening day, "an establishment containing the most modern hotel equipment and hygienic appliances to an extent without parallel in this part of the world". Acting Governor W.T. Southorn paid tribute to these efforts, saying: "No detail has been too small and no expenditure too great where the question of the health of the guests is concerned, and

Above, the first floor Tea Lounge opened on to a terrace, which would eventually become the Verandah; *left,* specialists from Shanghai were responsible for the interior decor

so far as human foresight can go, there can be no place in the world where the diner can eat his food with a greater faith in the purity of its preparation than in The Peninsula."

Lighting up The Peninsula was the largest electrical installation in the Far East. As one reporter described it, "The lighting and ventilation section of the installation is designed and laid out to supply no less than 2,000 points, supplying approximately 4,000 lamps of various candle power, 1,450 wall plug outlets and 185 ceiling fans." The Peninsula was also equipped with central heating, with radiators in all its public

rooms, corridors, bedrooms and bathrooms.

Central vacuuming was a great success; the centralised mail system somewhat less so – the collection chutes proved overly attractive to insects and the system was dismantled in the 1950s. The seven Waygood-Otis lifts (four for passengers, two for luggage and one for food) travelled 300 feet per minute and were run by trained operators.

The kitchens were treasure troves of modern, labour-saving devices. The dishwasher was equipped with automatic rack conveyors and could clean and rinse 18,000 pieces of crockery an hour. There were steam jacketed boiling pans, fish and pudding steamers, hot-plates, charcoal grills, gas grillers and toasters and gas cooking ranges. In the main kitchen, an electrically driven Hobart Mixer stood ready to mix 120 pounds of bread dough at one time, or 60 pounds of mashed potatoes, 25 quarts of mayonnaise or 16 quarts of whipped cream. A potato peeler, from Messrs. George Kent, Ltd., London, could denude 28 to 30 pounds of potatoes at one charge. There was even a machine which automatically cut and buttered slices of bread.

Fifty years later, the Hobart Mixer would still be mixing bread dough and mashing potatoes. But the bread and butter machine was just a memory.

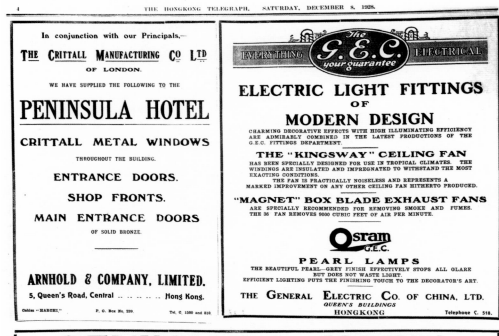

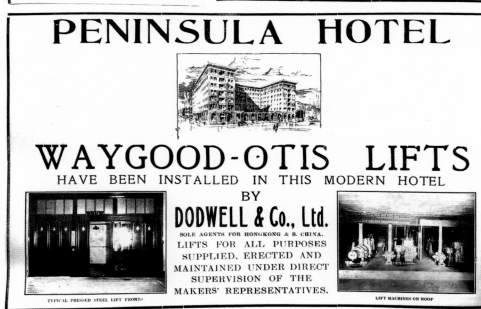

"R eady to Speed 'You' to Europe in 28 Days via Java" proclaimed the Java-China-Japan Line's 1932 advertisement. Compared to the various shipping routes available, rail travel was relatively speedy. Boarding a sumptuously outfitted train car at the Kowloon-Canton Railway, one settled in for a 10-day journey to London, via Beijing, Moscow, Berlin, Paris and Calais. Travel was necessarily leisurely in the 1920s and 1930s. Guests checking in at The Peninsula arrived with steamer trunks which unfolded to simulate not-so-portable wardrobes. The hotel's rooms were more like suites, including a separate boxroom, dressing room, bathroom, sitting room and bedroom. Guests stayed for weeks at a time, many of them resident elsewhere in Asia and seeking relief from the relentless tropical heat of Indonesia or Singapore or the colder weather of northern China.

The Peninsula soon became synonymous with Hong Kong

GEE! SO THIS IS HONGKONG AND THAT MUST BE THE PENINSULA HOTEL GEE!

THE pleasure that you see on their faces is real anticipation. They are looking forward to a good time.

Of course, if they were going away, they would appear just the same, only the pleasure would be that of reminiscence.

They would have had a good time.

Trust the Peninsula for that.

PENINSULA HOTEL HONG KONG

HONG KONG & SHANGHAI HOTELS, LIMITED
A. G. PIOVANELLI, Manager.   Acknowledgments to G.W.R.

Like a number of Hong Kong residents, Sir Horace Kadoorie called The Peninsula home. "At that time I was staying at the hotel, paying HK$11 per day which included four meals – breakfast, lunch, tea and dinner," he recalled. The menus were as expansive as the rooms: at least 12 dishes were offered for breakfast, while lunch called for a choice of two soups, fish, two main dishes (one hot, one cold). The dinner menu consisted of appetiser, soup (hot or cold), fish entrée, grill, dessert, cheese and coffee. Staff, meanwhile, earned HK$3.50 a month, including two meals a day. Free staff quarters were provided on the hotel roof, where, according to the then Captain of the Rose

Room, Tsui Tim, "we had all conveniences – hot and cold water, telephones and electricity. There was even a servant to look after the staff."

For all that The Peninsula had been built in the tradition of the great railway hotels of Europe, the hotel welcomed few travellers in its early days. Rooms were mostly occupied by expatriates whose employers' company homes and messes were already full to bursting. Tourists were rare in the 1920s. While the Great Depression was partly to blame, it was also true that savvy travellers preferred Shanghai, which was renowned for running the social gamut from sophisticated glamour to outright debauchery. In *Shanghai: Collision Point of Cultures*, Harriet Sergeant writes that: "No world cruise [in the 1920s and 1930s] was complete without a stop in the city. Its name evoked mystery, adventure and licence of every form."

But by the early 1930s, the Territory was a regular port of call for great ocean liners. The Peninsula's lively *Tavern Topics* magazine, introduced in 1932 to "accomplish the sometimes difficult task of amusing and entertaining our readers", reported the arrival in January 1933 of the *Empress of Britain*, which since leaving New York on December 3, 1932, had called at Mediterranean, Ceylonese, Indian and Straits ports. "She has all kinds of show people on board, G.B.S., Noel Coward, Cornelius Vanderbilt, Jr. (which stands for journalist, we suppose), and Princess Fe Ligne among others." Later in the same issue, G.B.S. was identified as "the great George

Gala events gravitated to the Rose Room

The main staircase, 1928

Bernard Shaw, who as usual we suppose will be as elusive to interview whilst here as he always is reputed to be".

It was the hosting of royalty, on April 26, 1929, that put The Peninsula on the top rung of Hong Kong's social ladder. For the banquet in honour of the Duke of Gloucester, and hosted by the Chamber of Commerce and China Association, the Rose Room was decorated with roses and violets and seating was arranged along a horseshoe table down three sides of the room. "All in all," approved the *South China Morning Post*, "the arrangements generally were excellent."

The Peninsula dramatically altered Hong Kong's social calendar. Party-goers rapidly adapted to the frequent necessity of taking either the Star Ferry or driving their vehicles on to the car ferry on their way to yet another extravagant evening at "The Pen". The St. Andrew's Society crossed the harbour in 1929, forsaking its traditional venue at the City Hall. By all accounts, the evening was a great success. Enthused one social writer, "Even from without, the hotel gave indications of the scenes of revelry within its walls. In striking contrast to its usual somewhat sombre appearance, The Peninsula was a blaze of light from floor to floor. From soon after nine o'clock, cars drew up in never-ending streams, rickshaw pullers puffed around the ornamented fountain before the entrance and disgorged scores of well gowned women, and kilted or tail-coated escorts."

For pomp and ceremony, the St. Andrew's Ball was impossible to top. The Governor and Lady Clementi were met by the Chieftain of the Society and escorted to the Ballroom where they were greeted by the General Committee. Pipers formed

Opening day festivities went on into the wee hours

up in front of the party and preceded them down the long corridor and into the Ballroom. Clan shields were carefully hung around the room and complicated customs surrounded the presenting of the haggis.

The hotel's manager, Mr. A.G. Piovanelli, catered to society's seemingly unquenchable thirst for novelty. 1930 was ushered in in grand style, with the Roof Garden glowing under an electrified "Happy New Year" greeting and the Rose Room the scene of a chariot race between the Old Year and the New Year, won by just seconds by 1930. One Christmas ball entered Hong Kong's popular history with its double-bill of four suckling pigs,

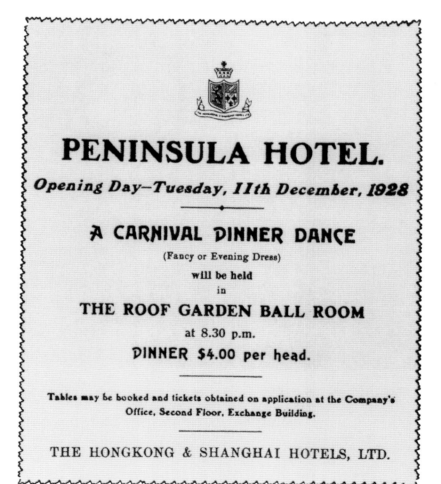

blue ribbons tied around their necks, let loose among the dancers, followed by Miss Dot Faye and Miss Valentine Arbisoff who jumped out of a huge rose on the stroke of midnight and proceeded to "perform a dainty dance".

Some of the more staid noses in the Territory sniffed at these goings-on and wondered *sotte voce* what the world was coming to. But ladies leaping from roses and the gaiety of The Peninsula's balls and tea dances, Sunday concerts, nightly dinners on the terrace and twice-weekly dances in the Rose Room did nothing to tarnish the hotel's reputation for respectability and propriety. "We always kept very high standards," said Chan Pak. "Unescorted

ladies and gentlemen were not allowed at the tea dances." And though the two sides of the Lobby were divided by more than a few feet – the west half being the province of people seeking romantic dalliance, while the only propositions discussed on the east side were of a business nature – woe betide the guest who tried to sneak a "friend" into his room. From manager to room attendant, the famed eagle eyes of The Peninsula staff conspired to foil all such attempts.

From Sir Robert and Lady Ho-Tung's splendid Golden Wedding party for over 1,000 guests in 1931 (upon learning that many of his guests had relieved the hotel of pieces of crockery and cutlery for souvenirs, Sir Robert reimbursed the management in full) to the Fanling Hunt Ball, the annual culmination of surely one of Hong Kong's most eccentric activities, with weekend fox hound chases after civet, paper or aniseed trails, The Peninsula reigned supreme. As the hotel's renown spread beyond the Territory, it was added to the itinerary of entertainers and tourists. In 1936, Hollywood arrived, in the form of

Charlie Chaplin and Paulette Goddard, stars of *Modern Times*, and Warner Oland, who played Charlie Chan. Before leaving his ship's quarters for a suite in the more gracious Peninsula, Chaplin held court for local press, deflecting questions about his rumoured engagement to Miss Goddard and satisfying the entreaties of a group of excited young autograph seekers. The stars graciously granted a similar request by The Peninsula and the hotel's celebrated guest comments book bore the first – and by no means the last – praises penned by stars of the stage and screen.

The Peninsula's ascent to the pinnacle of success and distinction made prophetic the final words spoken by His Excellency the Acting Governor W.T. Southorn in December, 1928: "The success of this hotel is not a thing of today or tomorrow. The inspiration which gave rise to this building is the inspiration of the future: it stands as an outward and visible testimony of the faith which is in us all; that the greatness of Hong Kong is in the future and not in the past."

Hotel staff pose for a pictorial souvenir prior to the opening

December 1928

AMAZING

GRACE

AMAZING GRACE

"There is a sort of war on, in the northerly parts of this China, and, quite recently, a slice of the earth's surface, as big as France, was transferred from the control of China to that of Japan – or something like that, we are told." And with this fleeting reference to the machinations building to a crescendo of war, the editor of the April 1933 edition of *Tavern Topics* moved briskly on to discuss Easter activities, expressing sympathy for those whose pockets would be lightened at the racetrack ("In Hong Kong we go racing, not a very joyful matter for the majority..."). Certainly, in some quarters there was apprehension concerning the effect on the Territory of Japan's 1933 seizure of Manchuria and establishment of the puppet kingdom of Manchuko, but Hong Kong, for the most part, felt safe and secure in its isolation.

As the decade matured, and with it the threat posed by Japan's inexorable move southward through China (after taking Beijing in 1937) this attitude persisted. Hong Kong's lively social scene simply accepted the insularity caused by the sudden lack of participants from beyond the Territory. Glittering socialites still filled The Peninsula's Ballroom and the band played on in the Roof Garden, but the staff had stopped looking out to sea in hopes of spying one of the ocean liners which used to signal an excited flurry of activity as Reception and Housekeeping prepared for the inevitable rush of glamorous guests. Even so, The Peninsula was by no means deserted. The 1937 bombing of Shanghai by the Japanese caused an influx of refugees which,

Preceding pages and left, the hotel's intricate decoration has survived the vicissitudes of war, occupation and time; *above,* the rickshaw and motor car were equally prominent in 1930s Hong Kong

company records noted, "taxed to the utmost the accommodations of The Hong Kong Hotel and The Peninsula". In the next two years, immigration would total 650,000. "The increase of the local population created additional revenues in local restaurants and cafés," added the report. At the 1939 annual meeting of The Hongkong and Shanghai Hotels, Limited, it was announced that the company had achieved a profit of over HK$1 million; "the first time in six years that the million dollar mark has been passed".

———◆·◆·◆———

Dorothy Kaucher was not a refugee, but rather a first-time adventurer blessed with a talent for unfortunate timing which aimed her maiden flight directly into the path of history. A struggling actress living in San Francisco, her deep passion for flying had grown since watching the *China Clipper* wing past the Golden Gate en route to the Philippines on its inaugural flight in 1935. In the summer of 1937 she could no longer deny this passion; she scraped together US$1,845 for a ticket

The sudden drop in tourism in the late 1930s brought silence to the Rose Room

to China and the Great Wall. As she recorded in *Wings Over Wake*, she and her several fellow passengers were alerted to the news of Shanghai's bombing while on that speck of a Pacific stopover, Wake Island. After being hastily vaccinated against cholera in Manila, she landed in a Territory preparing for a human deluge. At The Peninsula she was told, "Yes, there have been more bombings in the north. People are coming down from upriver. They're putting cots in the Rose Room here at the hotel." Alas, there was no room for her.

Kaucher, thoroughly intimidated, left the hotel "by tipping four bowing henchmen and a doorman. One of them put me in a car with an address of a possible room, and a Chinese driver who liked his own language best." After being rudely refused accommodation elsewhere and being deserted by the taxi driver, she was deposited in one rickshaw, her bags in another. "I fell asleep," she wrote. "They were still running when I woke up. Then, like homing pigeons, they headed right for the entrance – could it be – yes, there it stood, the entrance to The Peninsula hotel." This time, her request for a room was met with a smile and, more importantly, a key. She could only conclude that her experience on the streets of Hong Kong had turned her into the very picture of a refugee.

Ordinary rooms resembled today's suites, with a large sitting room and closets big enough for steamer trunks

Later that day, the traveller hired a hotel car to take her to the Island. With Car No. 32, Driver 91, she reasoned, "the world was primly turning on its axis. But I could not help wondering. Did these people in tea gowns at Kowloon, so calm, so sure, so amiable, did they intend to go on doing that in spite of bombs falling in Shanghai? Or did they look any more foolish than I, with rubbers and umbrella, in the eastern hemisphere?"

W ith the onset of war in Europe in September, 1939, Hong Kong was put on an official war footing and refugees began to look elsewhere for safe haven. "My first unforgettable stay in The Peninsula was in April to May of 1939," recalls Mrs. A. Lucille Hurley, of Spokane, Washington. "Japan was rapidly advancing down through China and with the exception of one or two actual residents, together with a few businessmen, we were the only guests in the hotel. Certainly there were no tourists."

Despite the palpable sense of crisis, Hong Kong residents seem to have viewed the circumstances of the late 1930s through a peculiar myopia. Christopher Isherwood, in *Journey to a War*, describes leaving Hong Kong with W.H. Auden on February 28, 1938, on the river-boat *Tai-Shan* (rather than via the Kowloon-Canton Railway, which suffered frequent bombing by the Japanese), bound for Canton. The first-time war correspondent had found the entire journey from London to be vague and unreal. Hong Kong had only maintained them in this limbo: "At Hong Kong, we said to each other, we shall wake up. Everything will come true. But we hadn't woken; only the dream had changed. The new dream was more confused than the old, less soothing, even slightly apprehensive. It was all about dinner parties at very long tables, and meetings with grotesquely famous newspaper characters – the British Ambassador, the Governor, Sir Victor Sassoon. We seemed to be in a perpetual hurry, struggling into our dinner-jackets, racing off in taxis to keep appointments for which we were already hopelessly late."

The management of The Hongkong and Shanghai Hotels, Limited viewed the conflict from two difficult vantage points: on the mainland, through its properties in Peking and Shanghai, and in Hong Kong. Recognising the threat, the directors of the company, now including Lawrence Kadoorie, met behind closed doors to draw up contingency plans in case of war and occupation. The company recorded at its 1939 annual meeting that, "with the advent of the war in Europe the tourist business ceased altogether in Hong Kong, and our usual business from transient guests was seriously affected". In June,

One month's accommodation cost HK$650 for a family of five; dining and sundry charges brought the grand total to HK$675.30

1940, the board shelved a plan to air-condition The Peninsula's Roof Garden and Jacobean Bar "in view of the present unsettled outlook due to war conditions". On July 1, 1940, the *Hong Kong Daily Press* announced that the Hong Kong War Effort Executive Committee Meeting would hold its first meeting at The Peninsula hotel at 5.30 pm. The following month, *Tavern Topics* suspended publication "temporarily, until evacuations are over and visitors are once again welcome to our shores".

The hotel had been the scene in November, 1940, of vigorous protests against the evacuation to Australia of expatriate women and children. "Husbands Protest", recorded the sympathetic *Daily Press*, in its description of the Rose Room meeting, where the Very Reverend J.L. Wilson, Dean of St. John's Cathedral, spoke to the assembled men. Even with Japanese forces occupying Chinese border villages and on duty at the Lo Wu Bridge, with France having fallen to Germany and the Battle of Britain raging, Hong Kong's husbands were adamant that their spouses had been sent away

unnecessarily. Incredibly, the pressure succeeded in stopping the evacuations, although the government stopped short of allowing those women and children already in Australia back into Hong Kong.

Along with meetings of the War Effort Executive Committee, The Peninsula was the scene of a multitude of fund-raising galas

If the Territory appeared to be dancing towards doom, it must be remembered that Hong Kong had never before been attacked, and that the conflict in Europe, for all that it had affected business in the East, seemed a far-off threat. Perhaps a stronger argument against panic was the mutual accord and respect which had existed between Hong Kong and Japan for many years. By 1941, even though blackout drills were regularly staged, firewood was rationed, and the Hong Kong Volunteer Defence Corps and auxiliary services were being mobilised, the seriousness of the danger had not penetrated people's consciousness. It was as if the war preparations were added to the list of diversions; pencilled into the calendar along with balls, races, vocal recitals, tea and dinner dances.

In 1941, the downturn in company fortunes was so severe that The Hongkong and Shanghai Hotels, Limited board member Sir Robert Ho-Tung proposed closing The Repulse Bay and The Peninsula hotels, or leasing them out, in order to mitigate losses already incurred. In electing to keep both properties open, the board unwittingly assured The Peninsula's place in history.

◄━•◆•◆•━►

On December 7, 1941, the Japanese attacked Pearl Harbour. As the skies over Hawaii rained destruction, 800 guests at the Fancy Dress Victory Ball sponsored by the Hong Kong Chinese Women's Club in aid of the British and Chinese Bomber Funds danced, drank, gossiped and cavorted in the Rose Room and Roof Garden of The Peninsula. "A brilliant function", according to the *South China Morning Post* the following day, unaware that its reporters were critiquing what came to be regarded as the last dance of the British Empire. There would be no leisurely reading of the newspapers over cups of tea that morning. At 5 am on December 8, Major General C.M. Maltby, Commander-in-Chief of the Far East, ordered the bridges at the frontier to be blown up. At 9 am, the Japanese launched an attack on Hong Kong and Malaya.

Instead of the expected naval offensive, Japanese planes swooped on Hong Kong, destroying the small RAF fleet stationed at Kai Tak. Then began a fierce blitz by infantry, cavalry, tanks and artillery. Three British battalions were charged with holding the Gindrinkers Line in the New Territories for at least a week, but within 48 hours, withdrawal from Kowloon was ordered and the soldiers were evacuated to Hong Kong Island. Under General Maltby's command were six battalions: two

British (the Royal Scots and the Middlesex Regiments), two Indian (the Rajputs and Punjabis) and two Canadian (the Winnipeg Grenadiers and the Royal Rifles of Canada). Also in support was the Hong Kong Volunteer Defence Corps, a multi-racial collection of men ranging in age between 19 and 65. Trea Wiltshire, in *Old Hong Kong*, captures the spirit of the volunteers, who "would quip that they had never held anything heavier than a glass of brandy and soda. Now they manned machine guns on mountainsides and faced a truly formidable foe."

On December 18, Japanese troops landed on Hong Kong Island. For the next week, General Maltby's forces struggled against impossible odds to repel the invaders. The hoped-for assistance from Chiang Kai-Shek's army did not materialise and the sinking of the Royal Navy's *Repulse* and *Prince of Wales* scuppered any chance of help from that quarter. The defenders of Hong Kong were mostly inexperienced, hampered by bad communications and a strategy that had not allowed for such a powerful enemy. Many instances of bravery were recorded, both by enlisted men and civilians. The Hong Kong Volunteers proved their talent for raising more than a glass: Scottish, Portuguese and Chinese companies fought alongside the regular troops and the Methuseliers, all aged over 55, held the North Point power station against repeated attacks, surrendering only when their ammunition was exhausted. Recognising the futility of fighting on, the Governor, Sir Mark Young, requested authority to surrender on December 21, but Winston Churchill had reversed his position that Hong Kong was impossible to defend and refused unequivocally to grant that authority: "We expect you to resist to the end. The honour of the Empire is in your hands." Finally, on Christmas Day, General Maltby informed Sir Mark Young that resistance was no longer possible and 15 minutes later the order to surrender was conveyed and the white flag went up on Government House.

On Christmas Evening, General Maltby and Sir Mark Young were escorted across the harbour, now a melancholy stretch of burned-out and half-sunk hulls, and strode into The Peninsula, where they formally surrendered to Lieutenant-General Sakai. The formalities dispensed with, General Maltby was taken immediately to a prisoner-of-war camp, while the Governor was placed in Room 336 of the hotel. He remained there for nearly two months, until February 17, 1942, when he was imprisoned in Woosung, near Shanghai.

━■━◆━◆━■━

At its last pre-war gathering, the board of The Hongkong and Shanghai Hotels, Limited noted the resignation of the Japanese manager of The Hong Kong Hotel's barber shop, "on the grounds of ill health". It was expected Japanese barbers working at The Peninsula and elsewhere in the Territory would follow suit. Quite unexpectedly, these men turned out to have been spies – The Hong Kong Hotel barber was, in fact, a naval commander – taking advantage of the congenial, informal atmosphere of haircuts and shaves to cull valuable information about the status of British forces.

The board's next meeting, scheduled for December 19, never took place. During the first days of the invasion, the hotel had been threatened by fierce fighting and finally all expatriate and some Chinese staff had boarded the last ferry to Hong Kong on the afternoon of December 13, by which time the British troops had evacuated Kowloon for the Island. Lawrence (later Lord) Kadoorie was one of the very last civilians to cross the harbour to the relative, and short-lived, safety of Hong Kong Island. The Defence Secretary gave him orders to retrieve his father, Sir Elly, from The Peninsula and blow up the power station situated at Hung Hom. The young Kadoorie refused unequivocally to make a move for the China Light & Power facility until he was issued passes for each and every one of the company's employees still on Kowloon. Conscious of Sir Elly's standing in the community, the military acquiesced and Lawrence made haste to cross the harbour. Forty years later, he told the story for a China Light & Power documentary: "When I got to Kowloon I commandeered a small bus and I drove first to the China Light & Power offices and continued to the power station. When I got there, I found that the instructions to blow up the turbine had already been given and that Mr. Gavriloff had done this. I proceeded back to the ferry. We managed to get on a steam launch and that was the last launch to cross." As he drove up the steep, winding road to his house on The Peak, his Sunbeam Talbot came under fire. After three-and-a-half years in a Shanghai internment camp, he would retrieve the car, *sans* wheels and with bullet holes to remind him of that dangerous drive.

Comprador of The Peninsula, Tsui Tim, found himself in charge. "Everything was left in my hands. Somebody had to control and run The Peninsula." Safer hands could not have been found. Tsui Tim had joined the company in 1919 as James Taggart's office boy and had risen through the ranks until he was in charge of all Chinese staff and catering. He was a past master at instilling order – an essential quality for survival in these chaotic times – and showed a deft inventiveness when unforeseen problems arose. For instance, although the management had heeded government instructions to stock extra food in preparation for the attack (there was an unprecedented 150 bags of rice, 300 bags of flour, each weighing close to 225 pounds, and 60 tons of meat in the stores), what the cooks were short of was salt. When it ran out, and people started coming down with diarrhoea, Tsui Tim had the staff open up pineapple hams preserved in salt and removed the salt for cooking. Feeding the more than 2,000 refugees, including 1,200 staff and their families, crowded into the hotel, was one problem. Protecting it from looters rampaging through Kowloon was another. Tsui Tim ordered the massive doors locked and barricaded and when that did not deter the mob, heavy objects thrown from the balconies did the trick. The Peninsula — minus a few tables and chairs — was secure. A less well-known story has it that the staff secreted a large portion of hotel silver somewhere on the second floor and, not content with simply putting it out of sight, placed a carpet of crystal glasses at the top of the main staircase each night, so that an intruder would be heard immediately.

Upon the surrender of Hong Kong, The Peninsula became the temporary headquarters of the Japanese army and the occupying navy took over The Hong Kong Hotel. While Sir Mark Young was being interrogated in Room 336, Tsui Tim was answering questions in Room 604. He had a Japanese soldier to thank for his release; the man, who had worked at the hotel as a barber, cum, spy, identified Tsui as "an honest worker", and he was pressed into service, this time co-ordinating the kitchens to cook for the 3,000 people in the hotel. Eight months later, he joined the exodus of Hong Kong Chinese being pushed across the border to lower the population (which eventually decreased by more than one million) and lighten demands on limited food and fuel supplies.

Not everyone crossed the border solely for refuge. During the occupation, Lindsay Ride formed an intelligence unit called the British Army Aid Group. In

At the Going Down of the Sun Oliver Lindsay describes one evening in October, 1942, when a member of BAAG helped two of the Territory's bankers, R.J.J. Fenwick, the Chief Accountant at The Hongkong and Shanghai Banking Corporation, and J.A.D. Morrison, to escape the Japanese. The three men had taken a tram to a beach where they were rowed to the mainland. Morrison wrote later: "We hadn't been walking for more than 15 minutes when suddenly and with no warning there was a rush and we found ourselves surrounded by about 15 armed men, looking down the barrels of rifles and revolvers. Fortunately the strangers turned out to be guerrillas, led by a former cook at The Peninsula hotel. I cannot speak too highly of them, and their kindness will always be remembered with deepest gratitude."

His Excellency Lieutenant-General Rensuke Isogai took up governorship of Hong Kong on February 21, 1942, when he gave a series of press conferences and interviews at his base, The Peninsula. The hotel was just a temporary measure for Isogai, until the builders finished adding Japanese decorative touches to Government House and its gardens.

———◆·◆·◆———

Postcard inviting travellers to the "Toa (East Asia) Hotel"; the newly-named hotel reopened on April 10, 1942

"By order of the Hong Kong Government we beg to announce that the establishment, Toa (East Asia) Hotel, formerly The Peninsula hotel, has opened for business as from April 10." The Public Notice, posted on April 23, 1942, promised: "First-class accommodation, excellent banquets; both European and Chinese food will be served for entertaining parties. Patrons are always welcome: Mr Takesiro Toki, proprietor." The hostile takeover of The Peninsula was complete.

Across the harbour, The Hong Kong Hotel had already been reopened, offering "afternoon tea, Chinese and Foreign dishes", including "Tempura grill in former snack bar". On May 4, 1943, The Hongkong and Shanghai Hotels, Limited's remaining property reopened under Japanese management, as the Midorihama (literally "Green Seashore Hotel"). Extensive renovation had been needed to remove all evidence of the heavy fighting that had raged in and around The Repulse Bay Hotel in those dark December days of 1941.

As it had done in peacetime, the re-named Peninsula once again claimed the spotlight. Conditions for many citizens were dire indeed, but the Territory's love of a good party survived intact and a lively social life was rapidly rejuvenated – to the surprise, even, of the new authorities. The Japanese-edited *Hong Kong News* voiced official consternation in February, 1943: "It is a matter of surprise, that during the Chinese New Year's holiday a well-known hotel in Hong Kong should have thought it fit to put on an exhibition of a form of amusement that smacked strongly of that western influence that Japanese efforts are striving to eliminate from the Greater East Asia Co-Prosperity Sphere." What had provoked this impassioned diatribe against an unidentified hotel? The fox-trot, apparently.

━━•◆•◆•━━

The Japanese accepted defeat on August 14, 1945. When the civilians in Stanley prison camp were freed a few days later, former Manager of The Peninsula, Australian Aubrey Dimond, made straight for the hotel and ordered the "Toa" sign removed. The public gesture signalled the end of the dark days of occupation and a new era of restoration. Dimond was joined by other Peninsula colleagues as staff filtered back to the hotel, many from the mainland, others from local restaurants and hotels where they had been sent to work by the Japanese.

The Kadoorie brothers, Lawrence and Horace, who had been interned in

Shanghai, made haste to ease the plight of refugees and to lend their efforts to rebuilding Hong Kong. "My father was the first civilian from Shanghai to return to Hong Kong after the war," recalls The Hon. Michael D. Kadoorie. "The family home in Shanghai had been preserved, because the Japanese thought it would make a fine house for their proposed puppet governor, Wang Ching-wei. When my family was released from the camp, the house became Allied headquarters. The first Allies to arrive were Americans. They brought K-rations and camp beds and resided in the house for several months, as did the crew of a British Halifax who had got lost." The bomber crew stayed four months; having limited contact with their bases in Kunming and Chungking, they flew according to the tapping of Mr. Kadoorie's great-aunt's finger on the barometer.

Desperate to get back to Hong Kong, Lawrence hitched a ride in the tail turret of the bomber, but the plane developed engine trouble and was forced to return to Shanghai. He managed to get a lift on a Kunming-bound Dakota, but getting any closer to his destination proved almost impossible. Finally, he tracked down an RAF plane scheduled to fly to Hong Kong a load of currency that had been sent from London to be used in putting the Territory back on its feet. When informed they weren't allowed to take passengers, the enterprising young man suggested, "What about freight? Take me as freight!" And so Lawrence Kadoorie flew back to Hong Kong sitting on a pile of bank notes.

"We were fortunate when we got back to Hong Kong in being able to prove ownership to institutions and shares which we had before the war, because the Japanese had not disturbed the deposits of those shares in the banks," recalled Lord Kadoorie many years later. "Consequently, it was possible to establish ownership to those shares and thus to the undertakings which they represented."

Lawrence Kadoorie said much later that the internment had turned his former deep involvement in philanthropy into a near obsession. After the war, he and his brother Horace worked with the Joint Distribution Committee, a leading Jewish refugee organisation, and arranged for the evacuation of some 14,000 Jews and 7,000 Catholics from Shanghai to Australia and elsewhere. Lothar Prager, now comfortably settled in Melbourne, was a young recipient of the Committee's, and the Kadoorie brothers' largesse. He was just eight years old when he and his parents were released from a prison camp in Shanghai.

"We went on an aircraft carrier from Shanghai to Hong Kong and there we were supposed to take up ships to Australia," he recalled. "But we were stuck because the Australian government had recalled all the troop ships to bring their soldiers home. So we were put up at The Peninsula for eight months." Prager chuckled, thinking of how that part of his story usually made people's jaws drop. He added truthfully and, he hastened to say, with great respect, "The Peninsula wasn't as it is today. The smaller children managed to get a room on the Mezzanine floor, where the shops are today. It was quite dark and dingy. The adults put up in the two ballrooms that were converted to dormitories. There were approximately 200 men in one ballroom and 200 women in the other."

Peninsula old-timers must have felt an eerie sense of *déjà-vu* in those first post-war months, for the hotel was requisitioned as the headquarters of the Kowloon Military Administration and once again housed British soldiers. "Although I have stayed at The Peninsula on 25 to 30 occasions over the past 48 years, its cool portals were never more welcome than in September, 1945 and for four or five months thereafter," said John C. Webb, then a senior bridge watchkeeping officer on board the flagship aircraft carrier *Indomitable*. Not everyone was as enamoured of the accommodation. One ex-prisoner of war wrote to the *South China Morning Post*, complaining that The Peninsula-dwellers had to subsist "on what is known as a sample diet. So far we have had no milk other than an invisible smear wiped past the bread before serving; no wholemeal bread, no chocolate, four duck's eggs in 11 days, no fresh fruit or anti-scorbutic substitute, no vitamin pills. ... In the prison camp, at least we had vitamin pills and three cigs per day for workers."

The former exodus to China was rapidly reversed and the population grew by some 100,000 people a month, burdening an already desperately short food supply. Officers were sent to Canton, Borneo, India and Japan to secure food and supplies. The government purchased items in bulk, provided free meals and imposed rationing and price controls. Ron Pascoe, of the aircraft carrier *HMS Slinger*, spent his first night in Hong Kong, in late August, 1945, at The Peninsula. His memories are of "four-course dinners (plus orchestra) and hotel service that most of us had only

dreamed about." The splendid meals no doubt helped him overlook the vermin also resident in The Peninsula: "Kowloon in 1945 had more rats than people," he recalled. His first or second night's sleep was disturbed by one of the creatures gnawing through his sturdy Navy hold-all to get at a bar of chocolate. This did not deter Mr. Pascoe from taking up residence at The Peninsula in 1952 when he joined Qantas's Hong Kong office.

Working with the Joint Distribution Committee, Lawrence (later Lord) Kadoorie helped evacuate thousands of refugees from Shanghai; The Peninsula's Ballroom was turned into a dormitory to shelter evacuees

Once again, The Peninsula was at the centre of the transfer of power. *The Telegraph* painted a picture of joy and relief: "Throughout the morning, the Kowloon peninsula was the scene of much excitement and jubilation. Packets and packets of firecrackers, hurled indiscriminately into the street from the upper floors of the houses in all districts, greeted the Japanese in their trek to the camp." Discussions between the Japanese and British on the handover of power took place at the hotel on September 3, 1945.

Mr. Webb described a city that was "starving and buildings were being torn apart for firewood to sell for food. I and many others came ashore to establish order, to provide protection for all major buildings, to provide power [initially a submarine was moored alongside the wharf to run the cooling water pumps and circulation pumps for the boilers], to recommence transportation, to cancel the yen and reprint the Hong Kong dollar."

The Peninsula contributed to a much-needed sense of normality early in the restoration period. At 3 pm on October 10, 1945, the hotel summoned all its resources, scattered and limited though they were, to stage the first post-war social function: a Victory Ball in the Rose Room, in support of the Chinese Relief and sponsored by San Mui Chu Youth Association. Peter Esdakoff's Band played, George Goncharoff's dancers performed, women and men, dressed in what finery they had been able to save or retrieve, shook off the close afternoon air to dance out their joy and relief at being alive. The timing was distinctly unusual (due to the curfew) and the refreshments produced by valiant chefs were a monument to ingenuity, but for a few glorious hours, The Pen felt like home; a little bruised, but definitely home.

Though The Peninsula had operated throughout the occupation, it was in dire need of repair. Chief Engineer Clifton Trigg had to cope with a gaping hole and water two feet deep in the basement; an ideal breeding ground for mosquitoes. "The army came in to help," he said. "They cleared all the water out and sealed all the leaks, and everything gradually got back to normal. But those mosquitoes were terrific!"

Company records describe this period as "Rehabilitation". Gradually, the room attendants, office boys, cooks, waiters and page boys trickled back to take up their pre-war posts. Men like Cheung To, who had joined the hotel in 1930; Yuen Po, known as "Turtle" because of his distinctive walk, whose first job at The Peninsula was as a page boy in 1934; Ho Shu, who had been inexplicably promoted from bedroom helper to *dim sum* cook by the Japanese; and, of course, Chan Pak, who had been employed at The Hong Kong Hotel until the difficult conditions there forced him to work as a hawker for the duration of the war. In the balm of familiar, if battered surroundings, the people of The Peninsula dedicated themselves to reviving the hotel and their lives.

Following pages, The Pen in the deceptive calm of the pre-war years; peace brought a new era and neither the hotel, nor Hong Kong, would be as tranquil again

Other Peninsula stalwarts contributed their efforts. Despite failing health, James Taggart returned briefly from the United States to assist the government in supervising the reorganisation of civil affairs and business. Horace Kadoorie also answered the government's call to civilian arms. In March, 1946, he went to Shanghai on behalf of the Civil Affairs Administration to negotiate with General Johnson of the US Army for surplus supplies for Hong Kong.

In June, 1946, The Peninsula was de-requisitioned, although for the rest of the year it, and every other hotel in Hong Kong, remained under emergency regulations. Hotel charges were strictly controlled. The price of meals was kept at the lowest possible rate – the "charge for military rations is well below cost price", according to the *South China Morning Post*.

Finally, on December 22, The Hongkong and Shanghai Hotels, Limited signalled its readiness for the limelight. The *Sunday Herald*'s Christmas supplement listed a stunning line-up of festivities at The Repulse Bay, Hong Kong and Peninsula hotels. With this invitation to reserve places at The Peninsula's Christmas Eve and New Year's dinner dances, the public knew that Hong Kong was not only back on its feet, but ready to dance.

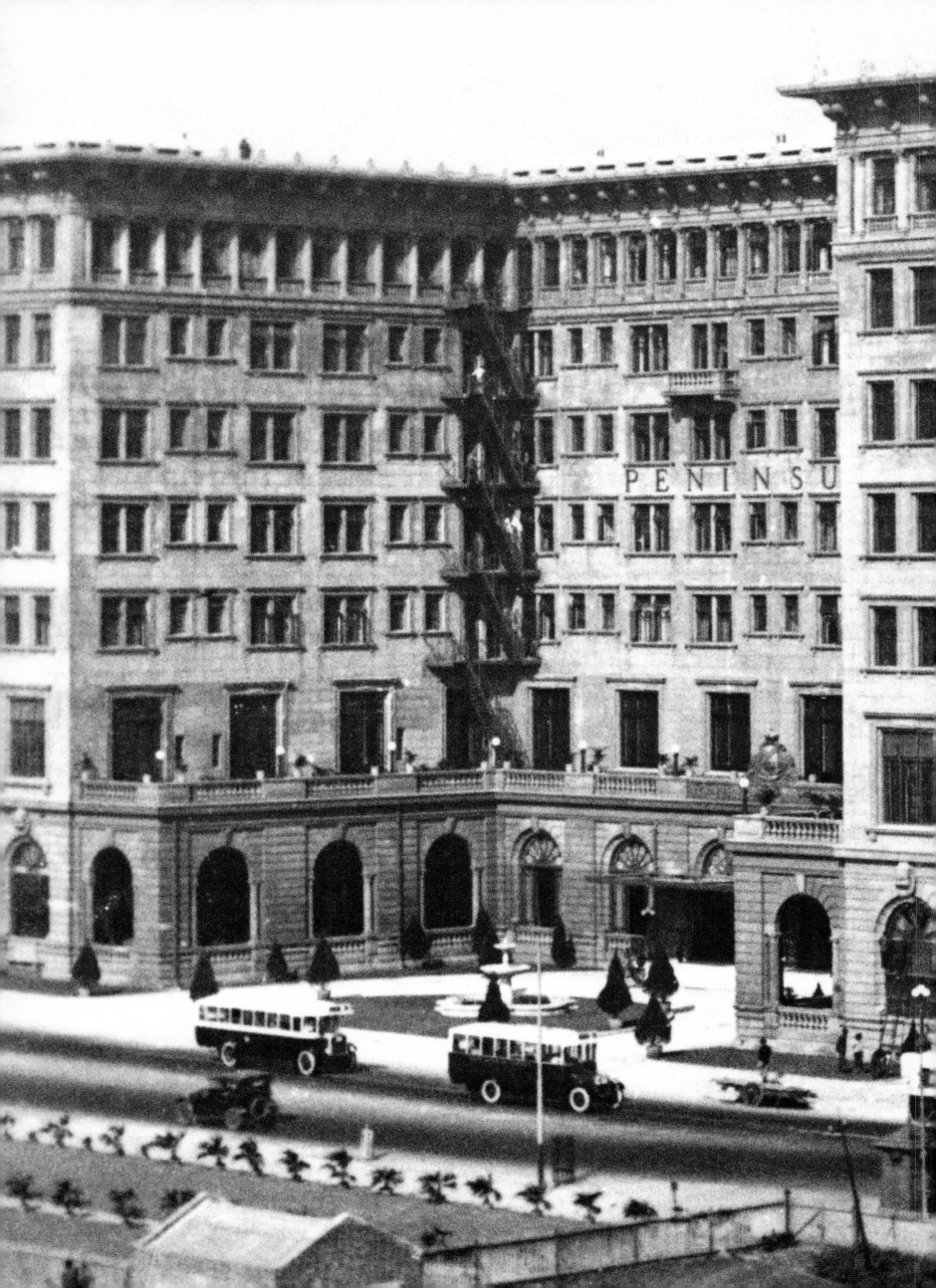

WELCOMING

WELCOMING THE WORLD

Preceding pages, view from the main staircase; *left,* buttons, gloves and shoes signal that these page boys posed in the 1950s; *below,* American artist John T. McCoy captured the *Philippine Clipper's* arrival in Hong Kong

Hong Kong entered the 1950s with a confident, even vivacious, spirit, buoyed by the speed with which the battered city had been resurrected. These were exciting, heady times. Prosperity was in the air, and there were no noses more talented at sniffing out lucrative ways to turn prospect into venture and opportunity into a deal.

Across the border, Chairman Mao Zedong had ascended to power, declaring on December 8, 1949, the formation of the People's Republic of China. Chiang Kai-shek and his Kuomintang followers had fled to Taiwan. The upheavals launched another massive wave of immigration across Lo Wu, but on January 3, 1950, in the *South China Morning Post,* Mr. Ko Cheuk-hung, MBE, Chairman of the Chinese Chamber of Commerce, spoke with undiluted optimism: "We can see that the situation in China is now

undergoing a great change, and it is a fact that no matter what form of government exists in a country, there is the necessity for development of her trade. We can therefore expect that better days and better opportunities for trade may be in store for us, probably in the very near future."

This optimism may have seemed misplaced. In large sections of Hong Kong Island and Kowloon, ramshackle squatter huts multiplied, carpeting steep hillsides and conquering formerly green valleys with clusters of corrugated tin.

Sir Jack Cater, who arrived in Hong Kong in November, 1945, with the Military Administration and then joined the civil service, eventually becoming Chief Secretary, recalled: "Textile giants came down from Shanghai and set up shop here in very difficult circumstances. They re-routed new, modern textile machinery which had been going to Shanghai from Cincinnati or Manchester and brought it to Hong

Kong. They also brought their managers and supervisors, and in no time the textile industry began to take off. Meanwhile we were experiencing frightful problems – the Korean War, the UN embargo, the American embargo on goods going into China – so we were going ahead with Hong Kong's industrial revolution with one hand tied behind our backs. And yet so successful were we that by 1956 the British were seeking discussions on quota controls on cotton textiles!"

When prominent couple, Mr. and Mrs. J.H. Ruttonjee, celebrated their 50th wedding anniversary, they chose The Pen

Like Hong Kong, The Peninsula had shed the youthful innocence that had characterised its pre-war days and was adapting to the opportunities posed by the increasingly international climate. It was in these post-war years that the hotel gained, and consistently confirmed, a worldwide reputation. With the 1953 closing of The Hong Kong Hotel, The Pen became the company's flagship, a status it holds today. In the two decades following post-war reconstruction, world-class restaurants were opened, levels of service achieved a popular fame and a measured renovation programme renewed the interior from top to bottom. As The Peninsula re-assumed its place as one of the grand hotels of the world, its management and the directors of The Hongkong and Shanghai Hotels, Limited, particularly Sir Horace Kadoorie, who would occupy the role of Chairman for 35 years, instituted change and growth with unerring confidence.

At the same time that Sir Horace was guiding The Peninsula into an era of great activity, he was also much occupied with the harsh conditions suffered by the Chinese immigrants who poured over the border in the early 1950s. Establishing the Kadoorie Agricultural Aid Association, Sir Horace, with his brother, supplied grants, subsidies and practical education to some 300,000 people, enabling them to become self-supporting farmers. In *Peddler in Paradise*, peripatetic salesman and regular guest Al Rabin praised the brothers' efforts on philanthropic and political fronts: "Farmers in this association now own their own acre, breed fine pigs, the best ducks and eggs in Hong Kong and are completely immune to Communism."

Deciding on one of the very first post-war alterations to the hotel must have been tortuous. While the camouflage paint was still being removed, the beautiful Rose Room, a gracious hall described as having "lovely, refined and restrained decoration", with an oval ceiling painted the shades of "the sky after rain", was sacrificed to the desperate need for accommodation. The resulting 40 rooms were known more prosaically as the Sky Terrace and were snapped up by British Overseas Airways Corporation (BOAC) for its flight crews. The design — or lack thereof — was dictated by expediency. Then station manager for BOAC crews, Richard Partridge, described them as "narrow rooms running from the corridor to the windows, made of fibre boarding. They had low ceilings, or false ceilings, and there was a shower only, a bed, minimum furniture…certainly no air-conditioning, no fans even."

Warm, impeccable service was at the heart of The Peninsula's red-carpet treatment

There were frequent skirmishes between the inhabitants of the Sky Terrace and a man whose appearance at The Peninsula marked the beginning of an era dominated by larger-than-life characters. Leo Gaddi had been a chef at The Hong Kong Hotel before the war. A Swiss neutral, he spent the occupation as a cook at the International Red Cross communal centre at Rosary Hill. Upon liberation, the company sent him to Shanghai to manage The Palace Hotel and supervise its sale and transfer. His exemplary running of that project was rewarded with the top job at The Peninsula. He took up the reins in 1948 and almost immediately found himself riding herd on the air crews, whose five-night stays tended to be heavily lubricated with alcohol. So much so, that the men and women would sometimes take their clothes off and race around. The problem was, they would sometimes forget where they were and hotel guests on other floors were occasionally startled by naked air crews running pell-mell down the hallway. Gaddi became famed — and feared — for his surprise patrols.

Below, as a personality and a hotelier, Leo Gaddi (in white) left an indelible mark on The Peninsula. Pictured here, Christmas 1958, with his wife, Frankie, Tsui Tim (*left*) and Ricky Vaterlaus (*right*)

Joseph Stuart Sykes, an American who frequently stayed at The Peninsula in the 1950s, recalled running into Leo Gaddi standing outside the main doors late one night, supervising one of the six-monthly fumigations of the Lobby. "Leo had been importuned by a streetwalker on Peking Road, abutting the hotel. Leo, of course, was supervising the fumigating and had stepped out for a breath of fresh air. After theoretically agreeing on a price, he asked the girl whether she wanted to go to her place, or to his room in The Peninsula. The lady said, 'Oh, I can't go in The Peninsula — Mr. Gaddi has thrown me out several times already!' Leo gave her HK$10 and a pat on the bottom, and sent her away."

But Leo Gaddi's reputation was built on more than his uncanny knack for surprising the mischievous mid-prank. He was a born hotelier who instilled strict new standards of service and shepherded the hotel through a period of great transformation. The beginning of his tenure coincided with advances in the aviation industry which reshaped the interior contours of the hotel. BOAC

was the first airline to consider opening a downtown terminal on Kowloon. Richard Partridge approached The Peninsula with a proposal; management cast an eye over the huge, tranquil (i.e. under-used) Lobby and agreed to shift the Moorish Bar and replace it with a passenger check-in desk. With minor construction and the hanging of a BOAC shingle, The Pen became the world's first city-centre check-in terminal.

The 1950s saw the arrival of two men who were to figure prominently in The Peninsula's development: Felix Bieger and Peter Gautschi. Felix Bieger was a chef on board a passenger liner plying the London – Japan route when he sought out chefs at The Pen, in hopes they had a recipe for a dessert called *bombe tango* which he was expected to make for a formal reception. He did not get the recipe but a job offer, and in 1954 he took up the position of Executive Chef with The Repulse Bay Hotel. It was the beginning of a 40-year plus career with the company, during which time Bieger would hold the position of General Manager of The Peninsula on three occasions. And, just as Sir Horace Kadoorie named a restaurant after Leo Gaddi, The Hon. Michael D. Kadoorie in 1994 announced that The Peninsula's contemporary, Philippe Starck-designed restaurant would bear the name 'Felix'. Mr. Kadoorie explained that the appellation was a "fitting tribute to a man whose immense dedication and loyalty have reached legendary status".

Top, Peter Gautschi succeeded Leo Gaddi; *above*, three-time General Manager, Felix Bieger

"I was 29 when I came out from Switzerland and I was virtually given the job then of being the future general manager of the hotel," reminisces Peter Gautschi. "When I entered Leo Gaddi's office, he stood up, slapped his chair and said, 'Mr. Gautschi, this chair is going to be yours in three years' time'." Looking back across 40 years, he remembers "a background where Communism was taking over just kilometres away, the Korean War had just ended, the Europeans knew their days were limited and Hong Kong was full of refugees. It was a unique scene."

━▪◆▪◆▪►

The approach to Kai Tak Aerodrome seems always to have been tricky. In *Aerial Vagabond*, Bessie Owens' account of piloting from London to Hong Kong, published in 1941, she writes of wicked down-drafts which almost turned her Waco over on her first approach. On her second, successful attempt, the gusts forced her to "pancake". The next day, the newspaper accounts described her as having "bounced" into Hong Kong; a description she agreed was entirely accurate. In his speech at The Peninsula's 1928 opening, Acting Governor W.T. Southorn had paid tribute to the burgeoning Territory, in particular its "fine modern aerodrome now under construction", but in an interview with the *South China Morning Post* in 1987, Mr. W. Hawke, the hotel's former butchery manager, recalled Kai Tak then as "just a mud field, and the only planes that landed there were Tiger Moths". In its early days, the runway crossed Kwun Tong Road, which would be closed, much like a railway crossing, when flights arrived or departed. The flying boats, of course, made no use of the runway. In *Wings Over Wake*, Dorothy Kaucher describes landing in a Sikorsky clipper: "There in a high wind, a Chinese woman in black coolie garb strongly rowed the boat that manipulated the landing ropes. I believe they called her Hongkong Annie." In the 1950s, the schedule of departures was dictated by the weather — planes could only lift off during the cooler part of the day, otherwise the wheels stuck to the scorching tarmac.

Heavier planes weathered the gusts, and the climate, a little better. By the time English novelist Ian Fleming, the creator of James Bond, visited Hong Kong in 1959 on assignment to write a travel book, *Thrilling Cities*, he was able to concentrate on the view, rather than whether he would live to write about it. Flying in on a

Left, the post-war boom in civil aviation brought an influx of new aircraft to Hong Kong, like this BOAC Douglas C-47, shown making a scheduled stop at Kai Tak Airport in 1948

Comet G/ADOK, "...we began to drift down to that last little strip of tarmac set in one of the most beautiful views of the world. It was nearly five o'clock and just over twenty-six hours and seven thousand miles from London. Twenty minutes late! Take a letter please, Miss Trueblood."

The flying boats, or clippers, landed in the harbour off Kai Tak amid a clutter of butterfly-winged junks, sampans, and ocean liners. Docking ropes were thrown and the craft was ignominiously hauled alongside. Passengers stepped out of the cabin, bleary-eyed from the days on board, and straight into the cosseting arms of The Peninsula. A hotel baggage carrier stacked the luggage on a cart, passport formalities were quickly dealt with in a mat-shed that stood in as the terminal and the visitors were ushered to a waiting bus for the five-kilometre trip to the hotel.

Residents of Kowloon grew accustomed to the throb of propellers and the sight of a clipper coming in for a sea landing, but the ocean liner still reigned. The Shipping List ran for four columns in the *South China Morning Post*'s Trade and Transport section in early 1950, accompanied by over three pages devoted to ads for a multitude of shipping lines. "Direct to London, Havre, Antwerp, Rotterdam and Hamburg via Straits, Colombo, Aden and Port Said," promised Ellerman Line. Klaveness Line covered the other side of the world with its 16-day journey to Los Angeles, "thence San Francisco, Vancouver, Seattle and Portland".

LOBBYING AT THE PENINSULA

It has been immortalised by novelists, journalists and travel writers, and captured on celluloid by Hollywood directors, but a late 1970s article in the *Asian Wall Street Journal* perhaps best encapsulates the appeal of The Peninsula Lobby: "At tea time, from 4 pm to 7 pm, it isn't the food that attracts the motley array of patrons...What attracts the clientele is the clientele."

In the beginning, it was the splendour which inspired odes to the Lobby. On opening day, December 11, 1928, *The China Mail* rhapsodised over the Italian Renaissance-style room: "This spacious hall with its enticing vistas in the perspective of immense piers, measures 52 feet by 150 feet, and is covered with mosaic tiles in a simple design in chocolate and cream...The ceiling of the Lobby is heavily enriched and supported by large square piers with finely-modelled bronze capitals." Some two decades later, the *New York Times* said, "The Lobby was wonderfully pukka sahib, a veritable stage-set out of something by Somerset Maugham. It was a delightful tall-ceilinged gin-sling type place where, one felt, rajahs must have strutted and European ladies followed by servants bearing steamer trunks would soon arrive for the season."

The Lobby

With its mahogany chandeliers and hypnotically whirling fans, the Lobby became a popular spot in which to enjoy a refreshing break. It was during the 1950s that, in a perfect reflection of the changing nature of Hong Kong, the Lobby metamorphosed from a quiet tea lounge into a lively, colourful "crossroads of the East" (this slogan was emblazoned on the sugar cube wrappers at the time). A fascinating panoply of high society folk and industrialists, White Russian refugees and Shanghainese textile barons, British and American military officers, high-flying financiers and film stars met and mingled under the placid gaze of the intricately carved cherubim and angels which decorated pillar and archway.

It was an environment designed to stimulate anecdotes and legends, and Lobby history does not disappoint. Here, Clark Gable, staying at the hotel while filming *Soldier of Fortune*, puzzled The Peninsula's barman by requesting, of all things, a tool. Seeing the look of incomprehension, Gable said, "You don't know what it is? It's the easiest drink in the world to make — I'll show you." He did and, according to Gable's student, Johnny Chung Kam-hung, still pouring drinks in the hotel's Service Bar, the screwdriver became *the* drink of the season. Here, too, the good-natured movie star was snubbed by a young autograph-seeking boy who confused him with another famous guest, William Boyd. "No, I don't want you, I want Hopalong Cassidy," the youth told Gable.

Some 30 years later, Richard Nixon would reveal an ironic sense of humour in the Lobby. On his way to the lifts, the former President of the United States spied a young tourist fiddling with a tape recorder he had just purchased. Making a detour for the lad, Nixon growled, "Be careful with that, son. One of those got me into big trouble."

Elton John inadvertently broke a Lobby rule when he tried to keep his trademark hat firmly in place. A waiter named Wong Wai, also known as "the bird man" because of his knowledge and love of birds, and who had no

idea who the musician was, asked him to comply with tradition. Elton John's polite, but firm reply ran something along the lines of "I'm Elton John and I never take off my hat." Wong Wai replied just as politely, "Well sir, I'm Wong Wai and when you're in my Lobby you really must take off your hat like all the other gentlemen." Bowing to Lobby etiquette and, not least, Wong Wai's charming insistence, Elton John did the gentlemanly thing.

A Hong Kong fashion designer fondly recalls the 1950s as the Lobby's heyday. She spent many an afternoon there, a young, inquisitive girl being treated to a club sandwich, which, to her great delight, was grandly served under a heavy silver cover, and ice cream by her aunt, into whose lap passers-by surreptitiously dropped pieces of jewellery, usually the property of down-and-out White Russians. These she would examine and, if she deemed them fine

Above, ornately garlanded pillar; *left*, "the crossroads of the East" was the haunt of high society, business tycoons, film stars and royalty

enough, she would convey them to a potential purchaser, either jeweller or a private collector, to convert to cash — for a small fee, naturally.

Propositions of all sorts were entertained in the Lobby. The late Lord Kadoorie once said to Leo Gaddi of the prostitutes: "If you have them, make sure you have the best." And at least they kept to one side of the room. The gracious centre aisle bisecting the Lobby is, in its own way, a demarcation as effective as a border or a body of water. The east side was the province of Hong Kong and hotel residents; travellers and people seeking "romantic dalliance" aligned themselves on the west side. The two quite different camps of women eyed each other with frank and friendly curiosity.

Three-time former General Manager, Felix Bieger, ensconced — where else? — on the east side, sketches a quick drawing on a paper napkin. "Then, the management offices were above Reception, overlooking the east side of the Lobby," he explains, drawing neat, half-moon circles to represent Leo Gaddi's and Tsui Tim's office windows. "Cable & Wireless and the airline offices were on the west side, with a bar running along the north-south wall. There was a lot of to-ing and fro-ing — who would want to sit over there?"

Who indeed? For starters, anyone wanting to stay out of the manager's sight. People like the Black Panther, so dubbed because of her predilection for black velvet clothes and a black turban. "The Black Panther's Auntie had a tailor's shop on the first floor," recalls The Hon. Michael D. Kadoorie. "She never wanted to stoop to lowly discussions about money. But she would saunter through the Lobby with her latest fellow on her arm, stop outside Auntie's shop and say, 'My, what a beautiful dress!' The guy would get the picture, offer to purchase it, and lo and behold, it fit her beautifully! He would pay an absolute fortune for the dress, and a week or so later, it would reappear in the shop window."

There were times when Leo Gaddi felt Auntie's actions strayed beyond the bounds of strict, Peninsula-style propriety and he would demand that the Chairman keep her in check, or better yet, throw her out on her ear. Shy and reserved, Sir Horace Kadoorie was also an uncommonly kind man, and his remonstrations were no match for the hand-wringing, tear-sodden performance that Auntie was capable of putting on in her ever-successful bid for sympathetic treatment. Many years later, long after Auntie, her protégé and her dress shop had disappeared from The Peninsula, Michael Kadoorie was in Los Angeles, meeting friends at a hotel on La Cienega, when who should come running up to him but the woman who caused Leo Gaddi and his uncle such distress. Having heard the stories and seen Auntie at her most flamboyant, he was taken aback when she asked whether she might have some shop space in The Peninsula Beverly Hills, due to open in several months. Familiar with his uncle's difficulties, Mr Kadoorie was happy to respond that, unfortunately, there was no available space.

Former General Manager Peter Gautschi held a contrary view of the Lobby. "I thought it was a little bit seedy," he says, recalling his first impression of the room over 40 years ago. "It had everything Kowloon needed, but things had been destroyed during the war, so you had a beautifully carved elegant chair next to a brownish glass-topped table and the chairs were covered in canvas. The hotel was the terminal — cargo came in, people bought tickets, there was a travel agency with a neon sign, people

delivering cables, crates of ducklings just standing there." In the early 1970s, under Gautschi's direction, the airline offices and travel agencies gradually found more suitable office premises and luxury brand names were enticed to take up space in the Lobby.

When a five-year renovation of The Peninsula was announced in the early 1960s, a Society for the Preservation of the Lobby was formed almost instantly. Its members' petitions threatened dire consequences if the trappings and the atmosphere were tampered with. "Word

came down from the management," says Peter Gautschi. "No drastic changes!" As one elderly lady watched the fans being dismantled, she said worriedly, "Don't you know how terribly hot it will be without those?" A staff member gently explained the properties of air-conditioning. The elaborate chandeliers and fans were excised, with the Austrian chandeliers attracting many offers. The ceiling was lowered to accommodate cooling units, the rather tired terrazzo was covered with a vivid tangerine

Opposite and above, the inspiration for the Lobby's magnificent scenes and elaborate decorations is a mystery; *left,* airline counters took over the west side of the Lobby in the 1950s

carpet woven to order by Tai Ping Carpet Factory and imported travertino toscano chiro Italian marble dignified the walking areas. The stained glass window that had illuminated the hotel's main foyer staircase was replaced with plain plate glass; its Rossetti-style maidens and cherubs were deemed out of place in the newly-modernised surroundings. There were rumblings about the loss of the glass cherubs and of the plaster angels who had looked out from lofty ceiling-high posts, but on the whole, habitués gave their grudging approval to the revamped Lobby. One can only imagine their reaction had they learned that one favoured suggestion was to divide the Lobby horizontally to add a mezzanine level.

This reshaping of its environment returned to the Lobby the grandeur which had been obscured, even dulled, by the bustle of flight announcements and rushes to the airport bus and lost if none of its irresistible cachet. Its reputation continued to precede it. Author and screenwriter S.J. Perelman wrote in 1975, "It used to be said of Shepheard's Hotel in Cairo that if one sat in its foyer long enough, everybody he'd ever known would pass before his eyes, which is why I spent all my time there in my room. I've done the same here, but for three different reasons — because the ladies in this lobby are too dazzling for mortal eyes, the pastries too much of a threat to the waistline, and the amenities upstairs and the courtesy of the staff unmatched in my experience."

Left, the beautifully renovated Lobby remains the heart of the contemporary Peninsula; *above,* restored gargoyle framed in gilt

The pretenders to the travel throne presented their services boldly. Cathay Pacific Airways offered "4 Engined Comfort, 4 Engined Speed, 4 Engined Security" on flights to Bangkok, Singapore and Saigon. "You Can Really 'Go To Bed'" assured SAS, extolling the pleasures of its luxurious DC6 sleepers, available on trips to Europe, Africa and the Americas. POAS (Pacific Overseas Airlines Siam Ltd.) directed all inquiries to "Peninsula Hotel Lobby; Tel 58865".

That line at the bottom of the POAS advertisement gives a glimmer of the radical metamorphosis of The Peninsula's Lobby from Tea Lounge to all-round travel centre. The Lobby branch of The Hongkong and Shanghai Banking Corporation had opened just days after the hotel did, in 1928. In the late 1940s, the bank was joined by Pan American, Cathay Pacific and Philippine Airlines, who opened check-in desks. Travel agencies, tailors and jewellery shops sprang up to serve the ready market and Cable & Wireless established its only Kowloon office in the arcade.

———◆◆◆———

Below, Mr. Angus Lee and (*right*) Mrs. Shia Ping Lee were among the first to take premises in the shopping arcade

"I sneaked into The Peninsula arcade," chuckled Angus Lee, of Falconer Jewellers Ltd. His first shop was in the Ambassador Hotel, but as The Pen's arcade expanded, Mr. Lee set his sights on the prime location. "The Peninsula didn't have any fine jewellers then," he said. "So I bought one of the shops that was already in the hotel and took it over when the owner retired." He quietly changed the sign to "Falconer" and replaced the medium-priced stock with exquisite jewellery of the finest quality.

"The Lalique shop used to be Philippine Airlines; Van Cleef & Arpels

was Air France; and I think Hermes was the TWA desk." Mrs. Shia Ping Lee, Chairman of Eileen Kershaw Ltd., Shiatos Ltd. and Shiamas Ltd., looks at the trio of luxury shops, but from the look on her face it's obvious that she is remembering another time. "Before, we had boutiques on three floors and I had to be up and down all day. It kept me fit!" It

was a time-consuming and delicate task Mr. Gautschi undertook, easing out the airlines and installing retail venues bearing upper crust brand names. It wasn't until the early 1970s that the lone hold-out, Philippine Airlines, finally decamped.

"The Peninsula is very strict," said Mr. Lee. "There is to be no cheating of the customers, and no sleeping or eating in the shops. Once, I put an American Express sticker on the door and Mr. Gautschi said, 'Oh my goodness! You have to follow The Peninsula rules!' I scraped it off and we got along fine."

◄─•◆◆•─►

Pierre Balmain used The Peninsula as a podium from which to dispense some blunt fashion statements during his visit in June 1965. The hotel magazine duly communicated the designer's informed dictum: "He did emphasise that cheongsams look delightful on the Chinese women, but that on the Europeans they just looked ridiculous — therefore, ladies, take the advice of an expert."

Famous signatures filled The Peninsula's register. The Lobby made its Hollywood debut in the mid-1950s production of *Soldier of Fortune*, starring Clark

Gable and Susan Hayward. According to frequent guest Donald Ellefsen, the movie crew developed a longing for home cooking and filled this need "by building a fire in the room and cooking sausage". Stars William Holden and Jennifer Jones stayed at the hotel while shooting the film version of Han Suyin's best-seller, *Love is a*

Throughout the 1960s, the glamour of Hollywood, beautifully personified by Elizabeth Taylor, was a frequent feature at The Pen

Many-Splendoured Thing. William Holden checked in again several years later, when he returned to Hong Kong to star with Nancy Kwan in *The World of Suzie Wong*. A ravishing Elizabeth Taylor stopped Lobby traffic in its tracks when she strode in with her husband, Michael Todd, in 1957.

There are guests who made indelible impressions on The Pen's staff, and who have pride of place in its history, but who, for reasons which shall become clear, remain nameless. There was the woman of ample proportions who let the water out of her bath, then attempted to exit the tub and became stuck fast, like a cork in a bottle. She managed to attract the attention of the astonished room attendant, who hastily summoned a doctor from the clinic on the first floor. His solution was creative rather than medical: the lady was extricated with the help of lavish amounts of soap and water poured down her back while two room attendants, one on each arm, pulled mightily.

One night in the late 1950s, a wealthy, well-connected tycoon failed to return to the hotel. His wife contacted the hotel manager and the American Consulate, with dire tales of a possible kidnapping. The resident manager rushed to the couple's suite, where he was joined by a Third Secretary from the Consulate, who had hurried to Kowloon by walla-walla — the only means of crossing the harbour once the Star Ferry had closed for the night. The concerned trio went to the Lobby, presumably to discuss what plan of action to take. As they were standing at the foot of the staircase, the massive main doors opened, and in walked the missing gentleman, clearly the worse for drink, followed by a young Chinese woman loudly complaining, "You have no pay! You have no pay!" The fellow stumbled across the Lobby and seeing his wife, turned to her and said, "Darling, have you got some cash on you?"

Ella Fitzgerald, Peter O'Toole, Kirk Douglas, Douglas Fairbanks, Jr. and Rex Harrison stayed at The Pen. Shirley MacLaine objected when Marco Polo Restaurant maître d' Ricky Vaterlaus added to her bill the cost of the silver chopstick holders that disappeared from her table as she dined, then laughed as she tipped her bag to show the disputed goods tucked inside. Candice Bergen graciously posed holding a cup containing a tea just introduced in the Lobby, "one of four believed to be new to Hong Kong — Chamomile, Lime, Mint and Rose Hip". Then Vice-President of the United States, Richard Nixon, stopped off during an extensive tour of the region. So did the man who made millions weep, *Love Story* producer Howard Minsky. The Peninsula was firmly entrenched as film set and celebrity haven. As jet travel became more affordable, Americans sought out the hotel made famous by its movie-star guests.

When Hong Kong's noonday gun went off a few seconds late one day in March, 1968, the man pulling the trigger was excused. Playwright, novelist, actor and singer Noel Coward had immortalised the gun in 1929, but even though he had already visited the Territory several times since, this was the first time he had been invited to re-enact those lines from the song he wrote while travelling by car from Saigon to Hanoi in 1929, *Mad Dogs and Englishmen.*

THE VOICE OF THE PENINSULA

"With this issue, your Hotel house magazine makes its first appearance for more than twenty-three years." It was November, 1963. The Peninsula had recently hired Dawn Burnett, its first Public Relations Manager, who was working on educating people about the job title and its function. "A lot of people seemed to equate 'public relations' with 'hostess', as in bar hostess, which created some confusion," she recalled. One of her tasks was to revive the in-house magazine which had suspended publication in August, 1940. "Temporarily," wrote the editor of that final edition of *Tavern Topics*, "until evacuations are over and visitors are once again welcome to our shores."

Tavern Topics made its debut in June of 1932. Its tone was informed and witty; its editorial direction clearly defined. "We shall keep constantly before us two classes of readers. The one who has spent the last few months

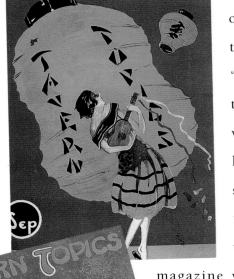

Above and right, Tavern Topics' mandate was to entertain both short-term guests and residents of the Territory who called The Peninsula home

in a tour of Europe or America and the other whose interests centre around this colony. We shall endeavour therefore to appeal to both. And so we ring up the curtain and make our bow. Salaam."

The ambitiousness of the task is evident in the contents of that first edition, which ranged from cultural exposés of jade and junks to "Tavern Wit" to a review of happenings and visitors at The Peninsula, The Hong Kong and The Repulse Bay hotels to tips for tourists.

Visually, *Tavern Topics* opened a window on the fashions, mores and trends of its period. The colourful, vibrant covers reflect the Jazz Age and the Flapper Era; advertisements

proclaimed the advantages of Roneo Office Equipment, "The most durable, best designed and best finished". The Peninsula also blows its own horn, describing, "Smart, prompt, willing service, on the part of staff…a magnificent situation and reasonable charges…good food in infinite variety."

Some 23 years later, the banner of the revived magazine read simply, *The Peninsula*. The new name better reflected the hotel's elegant style. As before, the publication focused on culture, Hong Kong scenery, events and developments in the hotel and its restaurants. Increasingly, too, it became a portfolio of celebrity names. In the over 30 years since its re-birth, the magazine has continually re-trained its editorial focus to interest and intrigue increasingly well-travelled readers and to provide a fascinating umbrella under which the spread of Peninsula hospitality is featured.

The title was changed to *The Peninsula Group Magazine* in the early 1970s when The Peninsula Group was created as the marketing arm for The Hongkong and Shanghai Hotels, Limited's interests around the world and the magazine adopted the classic A4 format in 1988. Throughout all the evolutions, the editor's brief remained true to the intent expressed in June, 1932: "We do not necessarily seek renown but we shall be most satisfied if we can accomplish the sometimes difficult task of amusing and entertaining our readers, and to attain this end we shall do our utmost to provide light and interesting reading material and the finest possible illustrative matter."

Above, the progression of a publication; *left*, *Tavern Topics* illustration from the early 1930s

The legend of the noonday gun was captured forever with these lines:

In Hong Kong

They strike a gong

And fire off a noonday gun

To reprimand each inmate

Who's in late.

While staying at The Peninsula, Mr. Coward spoke of his fascination with Hong Kong, saying, "Whenever I come here, I always take a front room at The Peninsula hotel where I can sit and look at Hong Kong Island and watch the ships in the harbour."

———•◆◆•———

"He serves Hong Kong best, who gives taps a rest." This slogan, penned in 1932, won a contest sponsored by the *Hongkong Telegraph*. Some 20 years later, much to the disgust of residents, visitors and the *Telegraph*'s publishers, who ran an irate editorial reminding government of its stale promises to do something about the water supply, the reminder was still necessary.

"We had perhaps three hours of water every third day, which The Peninsula augmented from a large tank on the roof," recalled Joseph Stuart Sykes, of California, a hotel resident in the 1950s. "For some strange reason, there was a plethora of summertime cocktail parties and receptions, all held, of course, at the then un-airconditioned Pen. The room boys would fill the bathtubs with water, which felt very good after a hot, sweaty day making travel agent and interline carrier calls." When the water was running, so were the room attendants — up and down the hallways, listening at doors to make sure guests hadn't inadvertently left the taps on before going out.

Providing enough water for guests' needs was a challenge for nearly four decades. During the 1930s, a truck would make the long journey between Kowloon and the south side of Hong Kong Island several times daily, where its tank would be filled with fresh water for The Peninsula from one of The Repulse Bay Hotel's three reservoirs. In the 1960s, water rationing was imposed almost annually. Mr. Harry Glazer of Montreal recalls having to rush back to the hotel between the hours of two and four to take a shower during the only hours that water was available. "We did, however, have a container of water in a barrel with a scoop so that we were able to wash ourselves."

In 1963, as Frank Welsh recounts in *A History of Hong Kong*: "Domestic taps received water only once every four days for one period of four hours, while stand-pipes in the streets, at which huge queues formed, were only open for an hour or two each day." To supplement the meagre supply, the Territory negotiated with China to provide 10,000 million gallons of water annually.

Extra measures were taken at The Peninsula, where management paid HK$35 for 1,000 gallons of water from the New Territories and built a storage tank in the basement so that guests could have water

Water was in short supply throughout the 1950s and 1960s, and strict rationing led to massive queues throughout the Territory

for one hour each morning and again in the evening. The problem was partially solved in 1963, when The Hongkong and Shanghai Hotels, Limited installed a HK$440,000 desalination plant at The Peninsula, capable of filtering and rendering drinkable 700 gallons of sea water an hour, and making it the only hotel able to maintain a 24-hour supply of water.

Guests looked out across parked cars and train tracks to the harbour

As The Peninsula's reputation grew worldwide, there was one aspect of the hotel which eclipsed the charm of the Lobby and the sumptuousness of the restaurants: the people. Time and again, a guest returning to Hong Kong after an absence of several years would be greeted by name — by the doorman, the Front Desk clerk, the lift operator. The Peninsula staff's remarkable dedication to service became legendary. One long-time guest, reflecting on twice-yearly visits over more than 30 years, said, "You know the best thing about this hotel? Every time we come back, they say 'welcome home'."

Mrs. Judith Heath, looking back on her first visit to The Pen, around 1950, remembers her amazement at the speed with which the room bell was answered. "I occasionally rang just to try to catch them out, but I never could," she wrote, "someone always seemed to be waiting right outside the door."

Peter Gautschi, who took over the Manager's role when Leo Gaddi retired, encountered in 1959 an amazed guest who hadn't been to the hotel since 1938 and happened to be staying on the same floor. The room boy had welcomed him back and called him by name. The guest asked, "Do you mean to say you remember me?" The attendant said, "I remember you very well, you had a problem with your knee."

It wasn't until the next morning that the sceptical gentleman remembered he had indeed strained his knee during his last visit and had it bandaged by the hotel doctor. "He apologised to the room boy for not believing him," added Gautschi. "This is perhaps extreme, but I heard stories like it so many times about staff recognising people and recognising what they wanted. Yes, it had to do with money, but pleasing the customer was absolutely tops."

They weren't angels, though. One of the room captains was a bookie on the side, before off-track betting was available. He hid the betting slips under the mattress of a bed in an unused room. In 1963, The Peninsula garnered unwelcome newspaper headlines when a gambling casino run by staff in their rooftop quarters was raided over Chinese New Year. "Half of Tsim Sha Tsui was up there," says Felix Bieger. That day, the alarm had been sounded twice (by a lookout knocking loudly on a pipe leading from the Lobby to the roof), but when both alarms turned out to be false, the third, real warning was completely ignored and police swooped down on the gamblers.

Older staff look back fondly on the quiet years, when the light work load gave them plenty of opportunity to indulge in marathon mahjong sessions that could last several days. Ironically, it was the youngsters who contravened the "No Football" regulation in the lane behind the hotel who were regularly brought in to the Tsim Sha Tsui police station. "These boys are from The Peninsula," the officer on duty would tell the arresting policeman. "Let them go."

New York Times correspondent, Craig Claiborne, was fascinated by The Pen's executive housekeeper, Nina Smirnoff. Born of Russian parents in Harbin, in northern China, she was a strong-willed woman who, when widowed in Hong Kong after the war, parlayed her fluency in Chinese into a career with the hotel. Claiborne was enthralled by her story about one of The Peninsula's room attendants who came to her one evening to say that a guest was repeatedly requesting a girl. "He telephones and says, 'Send me a girl. Send me a girl.'" Mrs. Smirnoff called the guest and asked discreetly if she could help him. "He said yes, he'd been trying for nearly an hour to order a bottle of San Miguel beer."

◆

During the 1950s and 1960s, The Peninsula carved out a sterling reputation for superb dining with, first, the opening of Gaddi's, followed by the Marco Polo Restaurant and Chesa. In responding to an unusual request from Swissair, the hotel also became the world's first air caterers in a venture that eventually led to the formation of Swire Air Caterers, in which The Hongkong and Shanghai Hotels, Limited was a 25 per cent shareholder.

"An evening bewitched with glamour," promised this advertisement for Gaddi's

According to The Hon. Michael D. Kadoorie, current Chairman of the hotel company, "Leo Gaddi came to my Uncle Horace and said, 'we want a first-class restaurant and we think we can do it'." Sir Horace had his doubts. "Leo Gaddi and my uncle had made a tour of Europe's great restaurants and, quite frankly, Sir Horace was not convinced that similarly high standards could be achieved in Hong Kong, due to the lack of fresh ingredients available locally. Fresh cream, an important element in cooking, was not available and the alternative of perishable Japanese non-salted butter, from which a form of cream could be made, could not be imported due to government health restrictions on dairy products." With a wink, Mr. Kadoorie adds that the hotel managed to "overcome" this difficulty, and the Japanese butter became a staple in the kitchen. Calling the restaurant "Gaddi's" was Sir Horace's inspiration: "He advised Leo Gaddi that the restaurant would be named after him," recalls Mr. Kadoorie. "Thus, the rise or fall of its fortunes would be tied to his name. Sir Horace felt assured of its eventual success."

Originally, the basement restaurant was decked out in rich, plush red and gold. Lady Kadoorie recalls, "We were in London and Sir Horace asked my husband to go to the hotel chinaware suppliers to buy for the new restaurant. The theme of Gaddi's, red and gold, was in honour of coronation year." Sir Horace, said his sister-in-law, was "rather a shy, retiring sort of person. The Peninsula was his baby. He was very thorough in his attention, very meticulous." Indeed, Sir Horace designed Gaddi's menus; the covers, with their satin embroidered Chinese figures, were a minor art form and "many a diner went off with one tucked under his arm," says Lady Kadoorie.

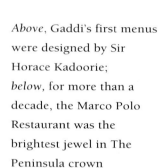

Gaddi's reputation developed straight away. The inaugural menus offered Russian, Chinese and Continental dishes. Later, Gaddi's was moved to the first floor, to replace the more prosaically named Main Dining Room. Chan Pak, whose career

Above, Gaddi's first menus were designed by Sir Horace Kadoorie; *below,* for more than a decade, the Marco Polo Restaurant was the brightest jewel in The Peninsula crown

had moved on considerably since his page boy days in 1928, had been Captain of the Main Dining Room since 1947. "I was the first Head Waiter at Gaddi's," he says proudly, "and I stayed there for 32 years."

Leo Gaddi supervised the menus himself and demanded only the best of ingredients. In 1954, he took a 22-strong team

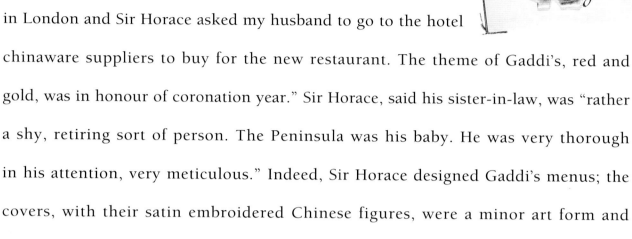

to Europe to participate in an international cookery exhibition and competition in Berne. They brought back a silver and two gold medals: one gold for the presentation of the menu, which has remained virtually unchanged; and the other for their sweet and sour pork. While in Berne, Gaddi took time out from the competition to treat

a young Michael Kadoorie, then attending school in Switzerland, to a helicopter ride. "It was my first ride in a helicopter," said Mr. Kadoorie, who recalls the experience which launched a lifelong fascination with aviation. A qualified helicopter pilot since 1973, he still remembers every detail, saying, "It was a Bell 47 helicopter and the ride cost all of 20 Swiss francs!"

Leo Gaddi took time out from winning one silver and two gold medals at a 1954 culinary competition in Berne, Switzerland, to take a young Michael Kadoorie, then on his half-term holidays, on his first helicopter ride

As well as providing an additional 90 rooms, most of them suites with kitchenettes, the 1956 opening of The Peninsula Court, directly behind the hotel, on Middle Road, opened up another culinary opportunity. No expense was spared in the creation of the Marco Polo Restaurant and from the day it opened in 1957 it outshone even Gaddi's for sheer lavishness. Local artist Francis Tsoy was commissioned to depict the Venetian explorer's journey on a fan-folded screen which stretched the circumference of the room.

As much as the food, it is the service which customers remember fondly — not surprisingly, as the restaurant opened with 54 waiters dancing attendance on 22 tables. Diners called upon maître d'hôtel Ricky Vaterlaus to grandly flambé dishes like Chicken à la Sue (chicken fillet on a bed of mushrooms, wrapped in foil) at their tables, basking in the intimate atmosphere and personal attention. It was a style not destined to last, but while it did, the Marco Polo gathered a dedicated coterie of followers.

When the Marco Polo Restaurant closed in 1968, Chesa had been putting Hong Kong's supposed intolerance of all things dairy to the test for three years. One might suspect that the opening of the restaurant was a plot on the part of the hotel's mainly Swiss managers to indulge a desire for home cooking. But, in fact, the roots of the venture lay in a 1963 Swiss promotion mounted by the hotel with Swissair. Overwhelmed by demand which forced guests to book several days in advance, the managers found it a simple matter to convince the board that a traditional Swiss restaurant was viable.

Cosy and warm, Chesa's decor reflects the personal efforts of General Manager Peter Gautschi and interior designer Dexter Yeh to achieve an authentic ambience. The pair toured Switzerland on a mission to source appropriate antiques and decorations, with Gautschi conducting a running lecture on Swiss culture to Yeh.

Swissair led The Peninsula to another culinary first when the airline's Hong Kong managers asked whether the hotel might provide hot meals for its flights out of the Territory. The chefs simply prepared gourmet meals similar to those served in Gaddi's for the delighted passengers on board Swissair's DC6Bs. It was quite a coup

Located directly behind the hotel, the 90-room Peninsula Court opened in 1957

in technical terms, as well. The Pen catered for the first two legs of the westbound journey: the first part, from Hong Kong to Bangkok, took five-and-a-half hours, while Bangkok to India was another four hours. All meals were served from a miniscule kitchen at 15,000 feet.

A long with modernising the antiquated billing system — consisting of a flimsy paper giving the total with a stack of chits attached — and implementing procedures to sell rooms more efficiently, Gautschi met the growing competition of the early 1960s head-on. As the Hilton, Mandarin and President buildings rose, with their combined 2,400 rooms, the directors of The Hongkong and Shanghai Hotels, Limited were convinced that a renovation of The Peninsula's faded 240 guest rooms and Lobby was in order.

The sweeping five-year, HK$26 million project, carried out by British architects Walter Marmorek and Peter Wormersley, was completed in 1967 and culminated with the transformation of the Main Dining Room into a Ballroom, something that had been lacking since the renovation of the rooftop Rose Room and Roof Garden

Gilded Door Gods placed at the main entrance protect guests and staff from footloose spirits

into guest rooms in 1946. The changes began outside The Peninsula, with a new 40-foot square fountain of hammered Italian Valentine granite and two granite Chinese guardian lions, so massive they had literally stopped traffic when they were delivered from Holt's Wharf at 4 am. Two Chinese door gods, painted on the plate glass doors, were the subject of an intense debate as architects and *feng shui* specialists (geomancers) wrangled over whether the gods' positioning ensured serenity or constant warring. On the roof, the employees sleeping quarters were completely renovated and a new staff canteen and uniform and changing rooms were provided in the service block.

The *New York Times* had made its feelings crystal clear when it published a cartoon of the Lobby with huge air-conditioning grills in the ceiling, streamers flowing from them, with a caption along the lines of "Things to come at The Peninsula in Hong Kong?" Fortunately, the outcome was more artistic and subtle than the cartoonist predicted. Luxurious carpeting and marble flooring replaced the terrazzo

mosaic and white columns met the ceiling in glorious bursts of gilded moulding.

The rooms were less successful. "No one liked the rooms," says Gautschi, bluntly, though he conceded that the marble bathrooms were a great improvement. The renovation brought a decidedly Scandinavian theme to the rooms, and with it, an overabundance of blond wood and red and orange carpeting and upholstery. The effect was modern, but somewhat sterile, reported newspapers at the time. Even so, the sumptuous Marco Polo Suite, boasting the largest sitting room of any hotel in Asia, won praise from its many celebrity occupants, though their comments did tend to focus more on the excellent personal butler than the surroundings. Similarly, it is difficult to be enthusiastic about the Ballroom: the room's gracefully moulded pillars were transformed to ones of stark beige marble, the newly-suspended ceiling sported gold wallpaper with panels of gold and silver leafite and the terrazzo tile flooring was replaced with an orange carpet.

Above, guest rooms were decorated with a Scandinavian touch in the five-year, HK$26 million renovation; *below*, the Verandah, 1965

The renovation sowed the seeds of another popular dining spot. Once an open balcony where guests enjoyed sundowners as they gazed across an unobstructed vista of Victoria, the Verandah had been enclosed in 1950 (and briefly named the Playpen) and now was destined to join Gaddi's and Chesa as a long-time favourite. Across from the Verandah, L'Apéritif Bar wooed crowds with Hong Kong's only organ. Further along the first

floor, two function rooms began catering for corporate events. At one point in the renovation, the Verandah was closed for ten days so that a massive cooker could be hoisted up through a window and moved into the kitchen. This marvel of stainless steel boasted four ovens, one bain-marie, two deep fryers, six hot plates, ten open burners, faucets for hot and cold water and a warming compartment.

When the last workmen finally downed tools, in March 1967, Sir Horace Kadoorie announced, "Four years ago, we were faced with a problem of the first magnitude: The Peninsula hotel, built in 1925, was about to lose its position as the premier hotel in the Orient. Competition from more youthful institutions could well have driven us down the slippery slope to oblivion." Paying tribute to the vision and hard work involved in the renovation, Sir Horace continued, "The success of their endeavours is demonstrated today in an atmosphere of luxury which could not be surpassed anywhere."

◆—◆—◆

Opening night at the Scene: when Michael D. Kadoorie proposed creating Hong Kong's first discotheque, half the board didn't know the meaning of the word

"It's quite a swinging place. A dimly glowing fish tank at one end filters a soft green light past finny things and shows up a round dance floor tucked in against the wall. Those who feel their way through the mysterious dark beyond the floor find plushy green chairs, little tables, a long white bar, and a large brown junk."

This account in *The Peninsula Group Magazine* of December, 1966 described the Scene, an innovation by the youngest member of the board.

Thirty years after making his first proposal to the board, The Hon. Michael D. Kadoorie smiles as he recalls that, "Half the directors didn't know what a discotheque meant and the other half didn't wish to know. One director looked me in the eye and said, 'every young director is allowed one mistake'." Even after the approval had been given, Sir Horace told him, "There's still time to back out." His nephew stood firm and the basement discotheque was a roaring success. With its own outside entrance, the Scene was about as far as possible from the formality that reigned in Gaddi's, which suited Hong Kong youth perfectly.

Hong Kong youth flocked to the Scene

Until the Scene was closed in 1977, to make way for new arcade shops, it lived up to its name. Its first anniversary was celebrated with a wild "San Francisco Night", creating "a resounding bang in HK's social whirl", as reported in *The Peninsula Group Magazine*. Make-believe hippies kitted out in flowers, beads, bells, tablecloths, caftans and shawls came to dance and compete for prizes. At first, a band alternated with a disc jockey, but for the last six years of its existence, the Scene was Hong Kong's only true discotheque.

The Peninsula Group had just begun to reap the benefits of these additional business ventures and the renovation when Hong Kong was affected by turmoil in China and war in Vietnam. When the 1966 riots protesting a proposed hike in the Star Ferry fares raged in Tsim Sha Tsui and Mong Kok, the hotel's doors and windows were boarded up, but because most of the staff lived in, all services operated as usual. Hong Kong and The Peninsula suffered serious fallout as a result of the 1967 riots, when activists of the Cultural Revolution then underway in China fomented dissention in the Territory. Scenes of rioting mobs, tanks on the streets and Government House being marched on by thousands were transmitted around the world. Mr. Martin

Trust, President of MAST Industries, who has come to Hong Kong on business since 1962, recalls the speed of the events: "It went from riots to major demonstrations, scattered shootings and great apprehension — with everyone thinking 'they're coming over the border' — and then it was over. It was compressed, it seems to me, into less than 100 hours." The memories took longer to fade, and so in 1968, *The Peninsula Group Magazine* waged its own propaganda campaign, reprinting articles written by journalists and travel writers debunking the myth that Hong Kong was on the brink of "becoming a miniature Vietnam, with Communist Chinese guerrillas scattered among the air-conditioned skyscrapers".

Once again, Hong Kong's ability to bounce back from hardship stood it in good stead. The Peninsula had survived riots, growing competition, typhoons and, not least, a tumultuous renovation that, in Horace Kadoorie's words, would allow "the duchess to survive to reign for many more long days". That "imponderable factor" – atmosphere – which in 1967 led *Esquire*'s veteran travel editor, Richard Joseph, to rank The Peninsula among his favourite hotels, was beautifully intact.

The Peninsula towers over a policeman directing traffic along Nathan and Salisbury Roads before the intersection merited traffic lights

RUMOUR and

REPRIEVE

RUMOUR AND REPRIEVE

The pendulum swings which for so long had sculpted Hong Kong's destiny as a refuge changed dramatically in the early 1970s. The clichéd description of the Territory as the "gateway to China" was still a twinkle in a journalist's eye, but its birth was imminent. Hong Kong woke to the realisation of the role it could play as a conduit for foreigners seeking a toehold in the world's largest market. An excellent infrastructure, sophisticated communications and a versatile business community which thrived in a *laissez-faire* environment were the best possible guarantees of success.

As significant as the gradual normalisation of relations between the United States and the People's Republic of China — Richard Nixon's 1972 eight-day visit to the mainland began the thaw, leading to the establishment of full diplomatic and trade ties five years later — was the 1978 announcement by then Communist Party Secretary Deng Xiaoping of a new "Open Door Policy". Suddenly, China was embracing outside investment, technology, management know-how and tourism. Hong Kong moved quickly to become the essential link between the mainland and the rest of the world.

A surge in visitors to Hong Kong was a natural consequence of this economic and political shift. The Peninsula's Reception desk was besieged by business people clamouring for rooms. In January, 1970, newspapers reported the erection of the framework for a bridge to connect The Peninsula Court to the hotel, described by a hotel spokesman as an effort to alleviate the "acute shortage of space in The Peninsula,

Preceding pages, long hidden by successive renovations, the woman dubbed "The Grand Old Lady" has been duplicated and placed in the Mezzanine; *left*, dramatic expansion plans would threaten the existence of the hotel and its most famous icons; *above*, the bridge linking the hotel and The Peninsula Court

which has recently been even unable to accommodate its regular clients". At the same time, The Peninsula Court suites were converted to guest rooms. Along with a music system and television capable of receiving "all four channels", The Peninsula Court rooms featured true luxury in the form of custom-made six-foot baths. General Manager Peter Gautschi, who proposed the link, said, "We put mock doors on the bridge and decorated it just like the hotel. People didn't even know they were walking into a different building." The HK$7 million step gave the hotel more than 300 rooms, a move which relieved Front Desk personnel, whose equanimity had been sorely tested by having to turn away so many regular patrons.

The company made another major investment in 1970 when director Michael D. Kadoorie placed an historic order for eight Rolls-Royces. It was the beginning of a long relationship with the British car maker. The association was interrupted briefly in 1974, but the switch to American Lincoln Continentals proved a brief dalliance, and in 1976 The Hongkong and Shanghai Hotels, Limited entered Rolls-Royce history for the second time by ordering eight Silver Shadows — the biggest single order on record.

———◆◆◆———

Hong Kong's development as the golden gateway to China was to prove the backdrop for a series of proposals, counter-proposals, announcements and retrenchments concerning the fate of The Peninsula. The extra rooms provided by the link between The Peninsula Court and the hotel alleviated the distress at Reception, but it was not a perfect solution. The viability of adapting a structure designed for a more graceful age to one which could offer the jet age traveller contemporary technology and style was questioned and debated with increasing intensity.

The 1970s were a time of diversification and expansion for the company, which was now marketed around the world under the name of The Peninsula Group.

A MEETING OF LEGENDS

One August day in 1995, The Peninsula's switchboard was besieged with calls about the hotel's Rolls-Royces. For once, the enquiries were not from reporters seeking information on the world's largest fleet of the British luxury vehicle, though no doubt the hotel's management fervently wished this was the case. No, these callers were hoping to purchase a decidedly damp "Roller".

During the torrential downpours released by Tropical Storm Helen earlier that month, rainwater had built up against the metal door of the new basement garage housing the cars, taking out the electricity to the waterproof pumps. "The door eventually bent and water rushed in," said then Fleet Vehicle Manager, Ken Richens. The flood level reached nearly four feet, drenching the nine Silver Spurs, but incredibly, stopping just inches short of the hotel's pride and joy, a 1934 Rolls-Royce Phantom II, fondly called "The Old Lady", which had been lovingly restored just a year before. The water-damaged cars were sold at auction and for nearly six months, until a brand new fleet of Silver Spur IIIs was delivered, The Peninsula's chauffeurs and guests had to make do with Volvos, BMWs and Mercedes-Benz. By then, floodgates had been installed in the garage.

The irony is that, pre-1994, there was no garage and the fleet, though continually exposed to the elements, had never suffered anything approaching this catastrophe. True, the chauffeurs caring for the first Rolls-Royces used a lot of elbow grease: the finish on the cars was vulnerable to water spots. The problem was exacerbated by the fountain of the time — in windy weather it had a tendency to spray just far enough to splatter the cars. An exasperated Felix Bieger finally installed a wind-controlled pump speed regulator on the overhang above the hotel's east entrance, so that if the wind rose or changed direction, the fountain's level would lower automatically.

The Peninsula's association with the venerable car manufacturer began in 1970. "The

Above, the magnificently restored 1934 Rolls-Royce Phantom II; *below,* Sir Horace Kadoorie accepts the ceremonial box of keys to another fleet of Rolls-Royces; *following pages,* flying past the skyline of Hong Kong Island, the Phantom presents a piquant contrast of new and old

board was looking at Harper Fords for The Peninsula," says The Hon. Michael D. Kadoorie, now Chairman of The Hongkong and Shanghai Hotels, Limited. "My father (Lord Kadoorie) said to me, 'Why not Rolls-Royces?' I responded that surely they were too expensive! 'Have you asked?' inquired my father. I hadn't and resolved to do so. As it happened, Rolls-Royces only cost 20 per cent more than the vehicles we were considering, so we took them."

Modifications have been made so that the vehicles meet The Peninsula's particular needs. The rear suspension is heavier, to accommodate passengers and luggage. The Silver Spurs feature vanity mirrors, reading lights and illuminated folding tables. Magazine racks which are pulled out of the back of the driver's seat were specially crafted by Park Ward, Rolls-Royce's coach building division. A small plaque on the armrest directs passengers to the built-in, insulated cool box, where they find chilled face towels. As well as a telephone for guests' use, the cars are equipped with a hands-free, trunked radio system, so that hotel and driver are in constant contact. Memory switches on a panel beside the driver's seat adjust the steering column, seat and mirrors to four different drivers' preferences.

The fleet which replaced the Lincoln Continentals was in a colour called Astrakhan Brown, as was the second order of Silver Shadows. Tradition returned in January, 1980, when nine Silver Shadow IIs, painted Brewster Green, arrived in Hong Kong. Before the cars were officially handed over to The Peninsula on January 25, the crest of The Hongkong and Shanghai Hotels, Limited was hand painted onto the rear doors at MD Motors Limited's Rolls-Royce Service Centre in Aberdeen. The deep, dignified green is now known as 'Peninsula Green' and appears only on cars intended for Hong Kong's Grand Old Lady.

Right, Lawrence Kadoorie and Michael D. Kadoorie celebrate The Pen's acquisition of Rolls-Royces; *below*, Rollers vintage and contemporary

Peter Gautschi was appointed General Manager of the Group's hotel and catering interests in 1970, together with Tony Oliver, General Manager–Finance and Administration. The two oversaw the Group's first post-war overseas interests and directed its movement into related business activities. In Hong Kong, The Peninsula Group had taken on the management of the new Hongkong Hotel in 1969, and in 1972, the Empress Hotel on Chatham Road also came under Peninsula management. The Peak Tower Restaurants Complex brought new focus to the top of Victoria Peak and Swire Air Caterers, for which the group provided catering management, produced up to 10,000 meals daily and catered for 75 per cent of all air traffic through Hong Kong. Overseas, the group signed management contracts with Singapore's five-star Marco Polo Hotel and with the new Peninsula Manila.

But it was the group's intentions toward its flagship in Hong Kong that attracted the lion's share of media and public attention. In 1972, The Kowloon-Canton Railway, which had played a pivotal role in determining The Peninsula's location, very nearly instigated its closure. The removal of the terminal was rumoured, then confirmed, and developers' eyes fixed on the spectacular waterfront site occupied by the tracks and terminus. Sir Horace Kadoorie, Chairman of The Hongkong and Shanghai Hotels, Limited, outlined a radical change in the company's corporate vision in its 1972 annual report. "Agreement has been reached in principle with New World Development Company Ltd., for your Company to rent part of the Holt's Wharf site." He outlined plans to construct one of the finest luxury hotels in the world, to be completed by the end of 1976. This new 500-room property would offer the service with which the name Peninsula was synonymous, but within surroundings designed for the modern consumer, who was considerably better-travelled and more demanding than the first era of guests in 1928.

Public reaction was swift and predictably horrified. The uproar over the Lobby renovation was a tempest in a teapot by comparison. One (unverified) story vividly told of an elderly lady's request to be informed of the date and time of demolition so that she could throw herself in front of the bulldozers. In a city where change is the only constant, where the eradication of gracious buildings which aren't living up to their plot ratio is merely a sign of progress, Hong Kong people balked at the thought of losing "their" Peninsula. The Pen was more than a landmark, it was part of a collective consciousness. Tourists may have been the hotel's *raison d'être*, but the local community was its heart. The Pen was where they celebrated weddings, shook hands on business deals, danced at fund-raisers, took their children to tiffin and *dim sum* and met their friends for jolly afternoons over tea or cocktails. There are few hotels in the world which can boast such wholehearted patronage; even though Hong Kong's social possibilities had expanded over the years, the community — Chinese and expatriate — looked to The Peninsula for style, for entertainment, for the best in food and drink. In short, for continuity.

The strong public sentiment was acknowledged by The Hongkong and Shanghai Hotels, Limited, but they recognised the challenges facing the ageing Peninsula, and practicality ruled the day. "A 'replacement' Peninsula hotel will dominate the Tsim Sha Tsui waterfront by 1977," reported the *South China Morning Post* in 1974. Chicago-based architects Skidmore, Owings & Merrill were appointed.

Work on the foundation of the "new" Peninsula began, and in a public announcement, Sir Horace gave more details. "In order to regain its past beauty and its rightful heritage, a new location 200 yards away has been chosen for The Peninsula." His assurances that the 17-storey edifice would faithfully incorporate "the vast Lobby, spacious guest rooms and as much of the old charm as is possible to recreate" did not allay the fears of the original hotel's devoted fans.

WEDNESDAY, APRIL 3, 1974

New Peninsula Hotel to be completed by 1977

A "replacement" Peninsula Hotel will dominate the Tsimshatsui waterfront by 1977.

To be built on part of the Holt's Wharf site, the new Peninsula will, however, retain much of the atmosphere of the existing one.

Foundation work is now being carried out on the project, jointly to be developed by the Hongkong and Shanghai Hotels Ltd – owner of the existing Peninsula – and the New World Development Co., owners of the site.

The General Manager of the Hongkong and Shanghai Hotels Ltd, Mr J.G. Oliver, said last night : "We're pressing ahead at full speed with the design and construction of the new hotel the replacement hotel will be much better than the existing Peninsula."

Demolition of the old Peninsula w' late 1977, following the completion one.

The site "'

and Shanghai Hotels Ltd.

"We don't know exactly what the redevelopment project will be, but it won't be another luxury hotel," Mr Oliver said.

The Chairman of the Tsimshatsui Kaifong Association, Mr Yu Look-yau, yesterday proposed that the Government swap a piece of land for the existing Peninsula.

"We would like the Government to preserve this landmark. The old Peninsula will be an ideal building for a museum and a cultural centre. It's a pity to see such a landmark come under the demolition hammer," he said.

· The piece of land · M· ' the one r~'

~'l

They have the oil crisis to thank for the fact that The Peninsula stood firm. On August 17, 1975, Sir Horace told reporters: "Quite simply, costs went up and tourism went down, so we decided it would be sensible to continue in the old way." The "old way" was found to be successful in terms of the bottom line: half-year figures for 1975 showed a rise in profits of 11.4 per cent. To say that sighs of relief echoed around the world would be fanciful, but not altogether untrue. The reprieve was welcome news, at home and abroad.

◄—•◆•—►

Life came full circle for Chan Pak when, on December 12, 1978, he presented a bouquet of flowers to Lady Maclehose during the formal celebrations of The Peninsula's 50th birthday. The former page boy's Peninsula career was as old as the hotel, and by the time of The Pen's Golden Jubilee, Chan Pak had been the captain of Gaddi's for 25 years. With the dotting of the lion's eye by the Governor, Sir Murray, later Lord Maclehose, the party for 4,000 commenced.

Champagne corks popped in merry syncopation to music by the police band. Pipers from the Brigade of Gurkhas performed with gusto. More than 800 dozen orchids and chrysanthemums filled the Lobby. "It was as if the hotel itself were dressing in its best finery to honour the cross-section of the community who had come to pay her homage on her birthday," reported the *South China Morning Post*.

The Peninsula turned 50 in grand style

Many areas of The Peninsula were indeed sporting a new outfit. Since taking the decision to retain the hotel in its original form, the group had lost no time in instituting a modernisation programme that encompassed everything from the logo to the shopping arcade.

CHAN PAK

"The story of this hotel is the story of Hong Kong," said Chan Pak. It is also his story. The elegant, silver-haired man, whom the staff call "Uncle Pak", grew up with The Peninsula. "My father was a seaman. When I was 12 years old, he lost his job. At that time, Hong Kong was a small island. There were only one or two big companies, so it was hard to get a job. My father couldn't send me to school, so his friends said, 'Why don't you send your boy to try for a job at The Peninsula?' My father brought me for an interview and I was taken up as a page boy." His salary was HK$1 per month.

Right, Chan Pak with Lord Kadoorie; *far right*, movie mogul Sir Run Run Shaw insists that Chan Pak oversee every Peninsula-catered function at his home

It was July, 1928. The battalions of Coldstream Guards and the Devonshire Regiment had left the hotel and workmen were struggling to ready the building for the grand opening in December. "We had nothing to do!" recalled Chan Pak. "Every morning the housekeeper brought me and nine other page boys to sweep the floors from the roof to the ground floor." He slept on the roof, in the staff dormitory. "I got two days off every month. I missed my family very much. But my mother came to the hotel to visit me. Back then, children had to take care of themselves, to build themselves up and establish themselves. It was very good here because the hotel staff lived at The Peninsula for the whole day, the whole month. It seemed like you had a brother or uncle there; a family."

Chan Pak was thrust into prominence on December 11, 1928, when he presented a large bouquet of bronze chrysanthemums to the wife of Acting Governor W.T. Southorn at The Peninsula's official opening ceremony. Plucked from the page boy ranks, the hotel's youngest employee wore what he called his "Prince Charming" suit — pristine white, with a white cap. Nerves and excitement served to turn the afternoon into a blur; all he knew was that he had performed his duty successfully.

Those early years at The Peninsula were quiet. Most of the guests were senior civil servants forced, albeit very happily, into residence at the hotel due to the lack of accommodation in the young Territory. Chan Pak began each day on the roof, scouring the horizon for the tell-tale puffs of smoke from an incoming steamer which signalled imminent guest arrivals. Nature dictated his promotion — when he outgrew his page boy uniform, he was transferred to be a waiter in the Senior Staff Dining Room and then to Room Service. "Then I went to work at the Roof Garden, the most elegant nightclub in the whole Far East. There was dinner and dancing to a nine-piece band," he reminisced. It was the era of tea dances and balls and Chan Pak worked at them all, learning the prescribed customs of the St. Andrew's Ball, the Hunt Ball, St. George's Ball and many other grand affairs. He recalls the post-war period when The Peninsula was the transportation centre of Hong Kong. "Every morning, we had people in the Lobby, waiting for their flights to be called. And the Verandah used to be only a verandah where people took the sun. There were stone tables and big sun umbrellas.

"In 1947, I became a Captain in the Main Dining Room. And in 1953, I was promoted to Head Waiter of Gaddi's." Standards of food and service were always exceptionally high at the renowned French restaurant. "When I was younger," he said, "we served caviar on a 50-pound block of ice — you had to hold the platter perfectly steady for guests." After 32 years of ministering to Gaddi's clientele, Chan Pak retired. "But I couldn't afford to retire completely," he said. "So the hotel offered me work as a Banqueting Officer." It's a role the venerable gentleman fulfils today, looking after private dinners and parties thrown by VIPs and long-time guests, many of whom insist on his presence,

saying that only Chan Pak knows how they like things to be arranged.

Smiling, he said, "Do you know how I learned to write? The telephone operators taught me. At that time, in 1928, they couldn't leave their posts to get food, so they asked if I would mind bringing it to them. 'Of course!' I said. I was a little boy, when I brought their lunch, they hugged me and put me on their laps and taught me some words."

Conservationists' heartstrings were tugged by the loss of the beautiful Ballroom in early 1978. But the venue was hampered by the large supporting pillars which rendered it unsuitable for most events and when an informal survey revealed that fewer than ten important social functions had been held there in the past three years, it was decided to move Gaddi's into the space. The Scene's disc jockey spun the last dance tune when the group opted to free up the 5,000 square feet it occupied for additional shops.

The unrelieved red of Gaddi's gave way to softer hues of light beige accented with gold. Tai Ping Carpets wove a specially designed creation of royal blue overlaid with a gold repeat pattern. The enormous pillars which had been such a disadvantage for a ballroom did not detract from the restaurant. The magnificent crystal chandeliers, imported from France for the hotel's opening in 1928, cast an evocative glow. Gaddi's clientele approved: Rolf Heiniger, maître d'hôtel since 1966, still presided over the most popular restaurant in Hong Kong.

The dated 1960s decor of L'Apéritif Bar disappeared and in its place the hotel unveiled a "gentleman's club". Green leather-buttoned armchairs, dark panelled walls enlivened by Chinese antique gouache paintings and heavy red velvet drapes combined to form a relaxed atmosphere. The Golden Pen and Golden Rule function rooms were also renovated.

General Manager Max Keller, who succeeded Felix Bieger in 1977 when he left Hong Kong to open The Peninsula Manila, explained the rationale behind the renovation: "The hotel must not be a museum. It must maintain its glamour, but at the same time be economically viable."

———◄•◆•►———

Months of speculation, theorising and rumour came to an end when the then British Prime Minister Margaret Thatcher and Communist Party leader

Deng Xiaoping put pen to treaty paper in 1984. Under the Joint Declaration, Britain agreed to return Hong Kong to China on June 30, 1997, and China agreed to preserve its social and economic systems for 50 years beyond that, in a unique "one country, two systems" approach. There were some jitters about how such an unusual condition could be achieved, but generally the business community responded favourably to the promise to preserve the status quo.

By 1987, tourism was Hong Kong's third largest foreign exchange earner. That year, revenue from tourism reached HK$25.4 billion and 4.5 million visitors to the Territory pushed arrivals figures 20 per cent higher than those for the previous year. Hotels naturally benefited from the unprecedented boom, recording 90 per cent average occupancy in 1987 and 1988. Their number had grown apace: the 49 hotels of 1978 had grown to 59 a decade later, and by 1991, an astounding 94 properties were expected to be open for business.

The cavalcade of celebrities continued; former US President Jimmy Carter is flanked by Peter Caprez and Urs Aeby

By the mid-1980s, The Pen was showing her age. Lynn Grebstad, Public Relations Manager from 1983 to 1986 said, "The Peninsula was like a lady-in-waiting; it was an old inn, but a caring old inn." Lynn and Urs Aeby, the then General Manager, still chuckle about the time former President of the United States Jimmy Carter came to stay. Not only did the Marco Polo Suite come in for a hasty repainting, "Lynn and Urs were on their hands and knees with blue markers colouring in the bare patches in the carpet," said Katie Aeby, adding that whenever the Marco Polo Suite was booked, she and her husband would loan their own Oriental carpets to improve the fading decor.

One of Urs Aeby's self-confessed claims to fame is that he nearly prevented one of the hotel's biggest successes. "Heinz Rizmann, our Food & Beverage Manager in the early 1980s, brought me the idea of afternoon tea," he said. "I'd tried to re-enact the tea dances at The Repulse Bay Hotel and they had failed. But I had already said no to several of Heinz's ideas and I realised I couldn't keep saying no. I told him, 'this is dead, it's passé'." He laughs at the memory. "It was truly successful and I nearly killed it!" Sultana-studded scones and wafer-thin cucumber sandwiches, served on elegant three-tier silver trays and accompanied by pots of Earl Grey or Ceylon tea (made with tea leaves, of course, not a tea bag in sight), was soon such a favourite ritual that people couldn't imagine the Lobby without it. The inaugural mid-afternoon feast set customers back all of HK$4.

Afternoon tea may be a relatively new institution, but an aura of tradition surrounds the trappings. The aged silver teapots are by the South Yorkshire firm of Roberts & Belk, which has been reproducing the same design of silverware and cutlery for the hotel since 1925. The imposing Christofle candelabras which lend such old-world presence and elegance to Gaddi's were brought to The Peninsula from Shanghai in the 1920s. A persistent legend clings to The Pen's silver; tales linger of a cache of plate supposedly tucked away in a hiding spot somewhere in the hotel as the Second World War descended, the location of which was lost forever in the turmoil of the occupation.

Author James Clavell (*left*) with *Noble House* principals, including Deborah Raffin and Pierce Brosnan

In 1981, the number of items in the silver storeroom increased by one with the return of an ornately decorated cake stand — 40 years after it was hired out. Wilfred Tyson's tenth birthday had been celebrated in the usual fashion; with a cake and stand delivered to his home in Kowloon Tong by The Peninsula. The stand would have been picked up the following Monday, but that Monday happened to be December 8, 1941, and staff at The Peninsula were too occupied by the Japanese invasion to think about the retrieval of a cake stand. It was put into storage by the Tyson family and forgotten. Almost 40 years later, as Mr. Tyson was sorting through his storeroom, he discovered the cake stand. "It was wrapped in newspaper and completely black. When I realised what it was, the memories came flooding back," he told reporters. That year, The Peninsula took up its pre-war catering role, complete with cake and said stand, and Mr. Tyson's 50th birthday was celebrated in fine Peninsula style, in the company of many of the friends who had wished him well all those years before.

In the 1980s, actors Pierce Brosnan and Deborah Raffin were filmed entering, exiting and walking through the Lobby for the mini-series of the late James Clavell's *Noble House*. "So many scenes took place in the Lobby that the producers re-created the entire room on a sound stage in North Carolina," said Miss Raffin. "It was meticulously done, the detail

Cake and champagne to celebrate the filming of *Noble House*

was perfectly duplicated. But they couldn't capture that marvellous atmosphere." Shooting in Hong Kong took place over ten weeks, and during that time, the actress frequently repaired to the Lobby, seeking out a quiet corner in which to enjoy a book and a cup of tea. In the Clavell saga, The Peninsula is thinly disguised as the Victoria and Albert Hotel. At a press conference held just before filming of the best-seller began, Clavell commented that "The Pen" was accorded a special place in his epic novel, as it was in the old wing that he wrote part of the book.

The Peninsula's propensity for renewal was very evident throughout the freewheeling 1980s. Some changes were initiated by the management and directors; others were imposed by circumstances beyond their control. An example of the former was the demolition of The Peninsula Court in 1982 to make way for The Kowloon Hotel. The basement of The Kowloon Hotel, which opened in February 1986, housed all the air-conditioning and other plants for The Peninsula to free up more sought-after shop space in what had become Hong Kong's largest accumulation of luxury boutiques.

A little over two years later, The Peninsula Boutique, conceived as the most specialised boutique in Southeast Asia and incorporating the famous Chocolate Shop, was opened. Then General Manager Eric Waldburger spent long hours with group President Onno Poortier, Vice President Peter Borer and a talented French consultant, devising a compelling and attractive range of products. Silverware, tea sets, bathrobes and cashmere pullovers were some of the first items on sale on opening day.

Mr. Waldburger had joined The Peninsula in 1987. Describing himself as "not the average Swiss", he applied an aggressive approach to breaking down entrenched, often inexplicable traditions. Discovering a storeroom piled high with old cake stands, trolleys and candelabras, he suggested that these marvellous pieces be used or displayed. "The staff said, 'We can't use them!', but they couldn't tell me why. I told them to polish and put them out the next day. I was like a kid in a toy store; I found things there that were absolutely incredible."

"Opening up the arcade was very clever," said Mrs. Mao Keen Ying, General Manager of Etro, who introduced the brand to Hong Kong with a shop in The Peninsula. Originally from Shanghai, Mrs. Mao's connection with The Pen began in 1949, when she and her husband moved into The Repulse Bay Hotel and frequented the Kowloon hotel's tea dances and dinners. Even though the couple relocated to Japan, Mrs. Mao observed the evolution of the hotel's retail collection closely. When, in 1986, a friend invited her to establish a market for Etro silks and fashions in Hong Kong, she approached The Peninsula for space.

"The match is a good one," she explained. The cultured, traditional style of the silk scarves and fashions is complemented by The Peninsula location. "I take my hat off to the management — they keep the colonial style, but they're always moving forward. Before I opened the shop, I always browsed in the hotel," she said. "And every night I eat dinner either in Spring Moon or Chesa."

A flurry of activity surrounded the first floor. Advertisements for Spring Moon promised "the magic of the Orient and a calm creativity, captured with charm, confidence and distinction". Specialising in Cantonese cuisine, Spring Moon was furnished opulently, with soft calming pastel hues and exotic antique displays. In its first years, the restaurant was under outside management; in 1990, The Peninsula

Cary Grant, Gregory Peck, Muhammed Ali and Telly Savalas hold a press conference at The Pen

took Spring Moon under its wing, bringing to it the same exacting care and skill which have made Gaddi's and Chesa's reputations unassailable.

Inagiku, the predecessor of today's Imasa, served Japanese food within an ambience that communicated the simple purity, delicacy and subtlety of Japanese style. The Verandah became a Grill Room: "French cuisine and the bounty of a charcoal grill, with a whisper of romance," read the promotional material.

The newspapers duly noted the new restaurant openings and reported the press conferences held by the unlikely trio of Cary Grant, Gregory Peck and Muhammed Ali (in Hong Kong to star as guests of the Macau Trotting Club, where races were named after them) and the more likely gathering of Pierce Brosnan, Deborah Raffin and James Clavell, on the eve of *Noble House* "action!" In the spring of 1987, however, real-life boardroom dramas dominated the business pages as The Hongkong and Shanghai Hotels, Limited, fought off the first of two hostile takeover attempts.

Corporate raiders launched an aggressive bid to gain control of a company whose portfolio included The Peninsula, The Kowloon Hotel, a string of international hotel management contracts (including The Peninsula Manila, The Portman Shanghai and The Garden Hotel in Guangzhou), the redeveloped Repulse Bay restaurants and soon-to-be-opened residential complex, The Peak Tram and the buildings at either end of the line, a wholly-owned subsidiary, Lucullus Food and Wines, a restaurant chain, 60 per cent of a dry cleaning firm and a 25 per cent stake in Swire Air Caterers. "We found ourselves in a takeover battle with those who had other plans for the land bank. We wished to retain the traditions of the Company with hotels and other property developments," said The Hon. Michael D. Kadoorie, Chairman.

The Peninsula's existence hung in the balance. Fascinated speculation about the bidder's intentions revolved around their lack of emotional investment in the hotel and the certain knowledge that, if redeveloped, the site could reap far greater financial returns. The battle for control of what brokers termed "the sleeping blue chip" ended after five months, only to be followed by a second unwelcome bid for possession of the hotel company. This, too, proved unsuccessful. When the dust settled, the Kadoorie family had maintained its leadership role and had increased its stake in Hongkong and Shanghai Hotels, Limited to 60 per cent. The silver lining in the corporate cloud was evident in the strengthening of the group as a corporate entity with a more focused direction.

———◆◆———

The Peninsula welcomed 3,000 revellers to its 60th birthday party on November 17, 1988. The Grand Old Lady was showing her age in places, but she was cloaked in a rich patina which had been burnished by luxurious, loving care. Her guest rooms had undergone extensive renovation in time for the Diamond Jubilee, as the previous ultra-modern decor, with its stainless steel and glass, had dated sooner than anticipated. Returning to classic elegance, rooms were furnished in olive green and terracotta, with walls in soft pastels and furniture of brass-trimmed burl and teak wood.

Presented with a huge anniversary cake, The Hon. Michael D. Kadoorie armed himself with a Gurkha *kukri* and made the first ceremonial slice. Actress Lauren Bacall joined in the festivities, as did Hong Kong tycoon Li Ka-shing, businessman Dickson Poon and British television personality Alan Whicker. Guests sipped champagne and nibbled on caviar in a Lobby festooned with fragrant lilies. The Gurkha Pipers played a march which had rung through The Peninsula on the opening day in 1928; an aural memory trigger for Lord Kadoorie and Chan Pak, both of whom had attended that famous occasion, 60 years before.

Frequent, long-staying guests Patricia and Colin Russell were at The Pen's Golden Jubilee, and later wrote of the occasion: "We watched in wonder throughout the day the beautiful flowers arriving from all over the world, the floral decorations, the magnificent ice carvings featured in the Lobby, and the pièce de résistance, the enormous array of Peninsula chocolates in the foyer of the Verandah! We laugh when we recall the many ladies of Hong Kong society with their handbags open, filling them with chocolates as inconspicuously as possible."

The celebratory mood was tinged with pride that the Grand Old Lady had sailed through the corporate commotion with her dignity and future intact. The Chairman of The Hongkong and Shanghai Hotels, Limited, The Hon. Michael D. Kadoorie, had confirmed rumours that the group planned an extension to the hotel and a model of the proposed twin-tower scheme had been unveiled. Events would bring the architects back to the drawing board for a fundamental re-working of the plans, but that was a few years away. As The Peninsula embarked on its seventh decade, the hotel continued to flourish under the steady hand of the family which had piloted its progress thus far.

ONWARD AND UPWARD

Dusk in the China Clipper is a magical time. Some afternoons, the fading sunlight paints the harbour in an intense hue of molten gold; other days, the cloud cover throws an intricate jigsaw of light and dark over the skyline. Whatever the climatic conditions, the sense of drama is potent. From this helipad lounge on the 30th floor, the vision behind the tower is suddenly, and vividly, comprehended. The Peninsula has not only reclaimed the singular loftiness which lent it such dignified presence during its first decades, it has done so with the same rare combination of dignity and spirit that made it a classic among grand hotels.

Preceding pages, a roof with a view: Hong Kong from the top of The Peninsula tower; *left*, taking in the panorama from the China Clipper; *below*, bird's-eye view of the Sun Terrace and main entrance

In character and execution, the China Clipper symbolises the contemporary Peninsula. Imagination and creativity, and no small amount of dedicated research, have gone into this superb facility in which the past and present coexist harmoniously. At once a salute to the early aviation pioneers who piloted Clipper flying boats,

linking Asia and North America, and a technologically advanced first-class helicopter arrival and departure area, equipped to handle international travel requirements, the China Clipper embodies the style with which The Peninsula has married tradition and progress.

———◆•◆•◆———

"**T**he Pen is not being knocked down but the old lady could have the fright of her life," was one reporter's assessment of the ambitious plans to erect twin towers on top of The Peninsula. A *Hongkong Standard* editorial, published in early 1987, asked anxiously: "What, we wonder, will we lose during this facelift? Will we lose the foyer, where one should be seen taking afternoon tea? Will we lose the exhausting but grand staircase which leads to the elegant restaurant? Will there still be room to glide up in one's vehicle and have it parked nearby by a white-hatted attendant?" All this and more, under the passionate admonishment, "Be gentle with the grand old lady of Tsim Sha Tsui." Before the year was out, a chance modification of the height restrictions on Kowloon had swept away the twin tower scheme, and with it, the worst of these apprehensions.

Above, the twin tower plans were replaced by the single tower scheme. (*right*)

Hong Kong-based Rocco Design Partners were appointed architects for the project in 1987. Their initial plans for two multi-storey towers involved filling in the gaps of the H-shaped footprint of The Peninsula with two blocks, joined by a roof terrace. "We developed this design to quite some detail and made a presentation to the board, which met with its approval," said architect Rocco Yim. Hong Kong's Antiquities Board had concurred, pronouncing it a very genuine attempt to preserve the character of the existing landmark and the project had moved to the tender stage when the Hong Kong Government unexpectedly expanded the parameters of possibility. The height restrictions on Kowloon, dictated by the close proximity to Kai Tak Airport, were modified in recognition of the less onerous overshoot requirements of modern jet aircraft. The plot ratio of sites further away from the airport was raised from 60 to 120 metres, and with it, the potential for The Peninsula to reach greater heights.

Whether one tower or two, The Peninsula's extension was more of a metamorphosis, fuelling the hotel's leap into a brave new era. The interior of the existing building had been reshaped, redone and remodelled so many times in the past 60-odd years that the original plans, had they still existed, would have been no more than curiosity pieces. The tower would ensure that the same fate would not befall The Pen. Ever-respectful, always tasteful, the rejuvenation of Hong Kong's Grand Old Lady would protect her past and guarantee her future. The provision of an additional 132 guest rooms and suites would be complemented by spectacular facilities: a Roman-style swimming pool and health spa, expansive function rooms, a thoroughly modern business centre, an innovative helipad lounge and a striking new restaurant.

Building a single, 30-storey tower would make it easier not only to keep the hotel operating during construction, but also to preserve the character of the old structure. Of course, "easier" is a relative term: there are inherent complexities in attaching a massive tower to an old edifice which itself has been renovated many times over the years. Coupled with the technical challenge was the human aspect. Minimising the disturbance to guests would continually test the capabilities of architects, contractors and, most of all, staff. Felix Bieger, who for the third time in his long career with the group had taken on the General Manager's role at The Peninsula, would draw on all his legendary charm and patience as he laboured to keep the staff motivated, the guests comfortable and the press informed. His over 40 years' experience with the company meant he was ideally placed to advise on both the temporary and final re-organisation of back- and front-of-house operations.

Faced with totally new criteria, Yim decided that, "we shouldn't simply mimic the existing façade. There were practical reasons: the room sizes and heights were different, the way the windows were to be designed was different, so even had

I wanted to copy the old building, I couldn't. We had to do it so that no one element was identical, but so that the combination gave it a very compatible, aesthetic quality."

The architect chose to use a unitised curtain wall system that could create a façade of similar texture and colour. The curtain wall units were prefabricated in Korea, with dies made in Switzerland, under stringent quality control standards, and fitted on site. The unusual texture was achieved with embossing. "We also used contemporary materials," Yim added. "We hope that, apart from achieving a compatibility between the new tower and the old, you can still distinguish that the new tower was built in the 1990s."

Originally, the Group had planned to follow the tower project with a complete renovation of the existing building, with a short breathing space between projects. But as the tower began to assert itself above Kowloon, the board weighed the impact of dust, noise and 1,000-strong construction crews, shuddered at the prospect of sentencing staff and customers to almost seven years of such commotion and decided that the renovation would run concurrently with the tower programme.

Work on what Neil McCallum would eventually describe as "the most complicated project" he'd ever worked on began in June, 1990. The first task was to clear a space for the foundation. The rear gap of the "H" had been filled with a three-storey building some decades before, and this had to be demolished. Unfortunately, the electricity supply, gas and all power came into the hotel through this addition. Worse, the water and the chilled water for the air conditioning was actually provided by The Kowloon Hotel via pipes travelling straight through this area. With no space for these services, either inside the hotel or on the ground around it, the architects looked upward for a solution. For four years, the transformer room that supplied power to the whole hotel was cantilevered off the side of the building in a steel structure suspended over Middle Road. A temporary network of pipes, which delivered the hotel's water, swarmed across the rear façade.

By the end of 1990, with the building services in place, albeit temporarily, the area was cleared and construction began on the foundation. A diaphragm wall was placed around the outside of the construction area prior to the excavation, then the piles which formed the foundation were built. As usual, because of the boulders common in Hong Kong soil, the caissons, or watertight chambers which surround the piles, were dug by hand.

Throughout 1991 and 1992, as the work on the foundations proceeded, the selection of interior design consultants took place. The English hotel specialist, Richmond International, which counts the recent renovation of London's Dorchester Hotel among its many projects, was chosen to design tower guest rooms and the public areas, such as the Lobby and function rooms; Denton Corker Marshall Interiors Ltd. in Hong Kong was responsible for the China Clipper and the health club; San Francisco-based Cuban designer Orlando Diaz-Azcuy was tasked with creating the concept for the swimming pool and roof terrace; and the design of The Peninsula's newest restaurant, Felix, was placed in the hands of eclectic French designer Philippe Starck. For the renovation of the existing building, local design firm PSI was appointed

to design guest rooms from a concept prepared by the group's in-house development team; Gaddi's, the Verandah and Spring Moon were handled by Brennan Beer Gorman Monk Interiors and the shopping arcades were revamped by Alison Henry Design.

Construction began with the demolition of a three-storey structure that had been added to the rear gap of the "H"-shaped hotel

THE EVOLUTION OF A HONG KONG PIONEER

Established in 1866, The Hongkong Hotels Limited was one of the first companies in the Territory to be granted a listing on the Hong Kong stock exchange. On December 1, 1892, The Hong Kong Hotel, the company's flagship, opened for business. A second property, The Repulse Bay Hotel, opened on New Year's Day in 1920.

The 1920s was a period of dynamic activity, not only in Hong Kong, but on the Chinese mainland. Plans for The Peninsula were set in motion in 1921, The Peak Hotel was purchased in 1922 and in 1923 the company took up 85 per cent of the issued capital of The Shanghai Hotels Limited, thus acquiring the Palace and Astor House hotels in Shanghai and a sizeable interest in the Grand Hotel des Wagon-Lits, Peking. In 1924, the purchase of the Majestic Hotel gave the company ownership of three of the most magnificent hotels in Shanghai. The registered office of The Shanghai Hotels was then transferred south to Hong Kong; the new company bore the name The Hongkong and Shanghai Hotels, Limited.

The 1928 opening of The Peninsula placed the company firmly on the world map of grand hoteliers. In the aftermath of the Second World War, The Hongkong and Shanghai Hotels, Limited dissolved its interests on the mainland, and with the 1953 closing of The Hong Kong Hotel, The Peninsula assumed the mantle of company flagship.

The Group's pioneering spirit continued with the formation of Air Caterers in 1967, the world's first air catering business. The Peak Tramways Co. Ltd. was acquired in 1971 and in 1972, the Peak Tower Restaurants Complex was inaugurated. Lucullus Food and Wines Co.,

development of a number of hotel, commercial and residential projects in North America and Asia. In 1990, The Palace Hotel, Beijing, was welcomed into the group. In Ho Chi Minh City, a commercial-cum-residential complex was added to the portfolio in December 1994. That same month, The Peninsula's spectacular tower extension and renovation were unveiled. In January 1997, The Thai Country Club was formally launched; Quail Lodge Resort and Golf Club in Carmel, California, was acquired just one month later. Peninsula tradition will soon open in Thailand, with The Peninsula Bangkok on the west bank of the Chao Phraya River, in Indonesia with The Peninsula Jakarta and in Sydney, Australia.

Left, The Peninsula Manila; *above*, the flagship Hong Kong Hotel was one of the Territory's first hostelries; *below*, The Peak Tram

a retail and wholesale supplier of quality foods and beverages, was formed in 1977.

The Peninsula Manila opened in 1976, and The Kowloon Hotel a decade later. In 1988, the group entered the North American market, with the acquisition of The Peninsula New York, followed by The Sutton serviced apartments in New York in 1990 and The Peninsula Beverly Hills in 1991. The company has since initiated

"We may be the oldest hotel company in Asia, but we're a young company, with all the dynamism and forward-thinking that that suggests," said The Hon. Michael D. Kadoorie of the business in which his family has been involved since the turn of the century.

Top-down construction began in February, 1992. Just over a year later, the tower had risen to its full height of 30 storeys. On May 19, 1993, under a brilliant blue sky dotted with puffs of cloud and the watchful lenses of a press gallery, Lord Kadoorie, assisted by his grandson, Philip, performed the topping-out ceremony. He was accompanied by other members of the family, including Lady Kadoorie, Sir Horace Kadoorie and The Hon. Michael D. and Mrs. Betty Kadoorie. Beyond the red-carpeted rooftop, Victoria Harbour glowed jade-green in contrast to the glittering silver and gold skyline lining the shore. The magnitude of the tower and its implications for The Peninsula were gloriously evident. It was a day of great consequence for the Kadoorie family. Lord Kadoorie, Chairman of the hotel company from 1946–1950, who had attended the hotel's ground-breaking and opening ceremonies more than 65 years before, and his younger brother, Sir Horace, who had lived at the hotel in the late 1920s and was the group's Chairman for 35 years, becoming Honorary Life President when he retired from the chair in 1985, glimpsed the future through the eyes of their son and nephew, respectively.

As the tower took shape over Kowloon, staff and guests coped with moving kitchens, half a Lobby and occasional lapses in electricity

———◆·◆·◆———

"It was like being attacked on all sides," said Executive Chef, Florian Trento, "but we survived four years of upheaval with no major disasters." The battle began with the closing of the old Main Kitchen; the smaller Gaddi's Kitchen served all the outlets. Chefs cooked wherever there was space — on tables in the corridor, at one point. When the Production Kitchen, the first to be opened in the new tower, was ready for operation, chefs matter-of-factly closed some of the massive soup kettles, placed gas grills on the lids, hooked up the grills to bottles of gas and began sautéing. When the Pastry Kitchen was closed with just two days warning, cakes and desserts were mixed, shaped and decorated on a table in the corner of the crowded Production Kitchen. For most of the two years that the Lobby was under renovation, waiters bumped shoulders as they collected their orders from a temporary kitchen located in what is now the Cartier shop. Pots and pans were stored in vacant guest rooms, which worked well, though there was always a bit of panic when new equipment arrived before its final destination was ready. "Gaddi's was closed for eight months and we made changes to the other menus, offering buffets and fewer main courses," said Chef Trento. "What we did, we did well."

"There came a time very near the end when we ran a 40-room hotel, with half a Lobby and one restaurant and 700 staff and 1,000 people on the construction site," recalled Peter Borer, adding with commendable understatement; "That was chaotic." Heavy rainstorms complicated matters. The worst deluge struck in early 1994. "Within half an hour the entire roof had flooded and the water went throughout the building, all the way down to the kitchen, and hit a major gas distribution pipe," he said. "That day, The Pen served cold lunch."

Some of the chaos and many of the delays could have been avoided, had the hotel been closed for the duration. The Peninsula, however, remained open, for one very simple, very important reason. "We have wonderful, loyal staff and it would have been a tragedy to risk losing them," said William E. Mocatta, Deputy Chairman of The Hongkong and Shanghai Hotels, Limited and head of the Central Finance Committee. "It was not a difficult decision," he explained. Recalling those taxing months, he smiled and added, "When there is a lot of noise and construction upheaval,

Lord Kadoorie performed the topping-out ceremony, assisted by his grandson Philip. Other members of his family, included Lady Kadoorie, Sir Horace Kadoorie, his daughter The Hon. Rita McAulay and her husband Mr. Ronald McAulay, a director of the company. Also in attendance were The Hon. Michael D. Kadoorie and Mrs. Betty Kadoorie, with Philip's sisters Natalie and Bettina

the more staff you have to appease guests the better."

Amazingly, guests tended to be intrigued, rather than infuriated, by the construction process. Peninsula regulars, many of whom make two trips to the hotel each year and who account for almost 50 per cent of total visitors, were fascinated by all the transformations that had taken place since they had last checked in. "On one visit, guests would arrive through the main doors," said Michael Hoffmann, then Resident Manager, "the next time, they would be coming in through the Lobby windows."

At various stages of the construction, one special outside consultant was called on. Choy Park Lai, a *fung shui* man, or geomancer, for 50 years, visited the site on numerous occasions to recommend the most auspicious placement of not only doors, desks and chairs, but the hotel's Reception. "From 1984 to 2003, having the Reception desk face east will give the greatest benefit," he said. Mr. Choy also fixed the date for the extension's grand opening ceremony, according to the formulas of his science, which take into account the hotel's location, the direction it faces and the birthdate of The Hon Michael D. Kadoorie. The combination of these factors led Mr. Choy to advise opening the tower on December 1, 1994, so as to maximise profit and prosperity.

◄─•◆•─►

Plump cherubs floating at her feet and garlands of flowers tracing a virtuous path across her nude body, the forever-youthful grand old lady of The Peninsula gazes with unseeing eyes across the function room foyer. If truth be told, the figure bounded by glassed-in displays of original Gaddi's chinaware, silver salvers and reservation stands dating from 1928 is actually the lady's contemporary double; a near-perfect copy of the long-forgotten original, which still languishes in total darkness on the other side of the wall. It was Richmond's David Buffery who made the discovery after clambering through the hole which gave workmen access to the current ceiling for purposes of air-conditioning installation. Standing on the catwalk and looking at the Lobby ceiling with which the hotel had opened, he took a good look around and saw what everyone else had missed. "We tried to get her off the wall, but it was impossible," he said. "So we took two rubber moulds, cast her in the function room and put her on the Mezzanine wall." An artist applied an authentic-looking patina of age, hiding the minute line where the moulds met. Beneath her,

the decorative flowers are copies of those which danced around the top of the original scene; the original bottom section had been hacked away years ago.

This reproduction was made of the original treasure, which was revealed during the Lobby renovation

The identity of the woman Buffery dubbed "the grand old lady" is as much a mystery as the gargoyles and other Lobby figures. They were created by master craftsmen from Shanghai; beyond that, no one knows who, or what literary works, if any, they were modelled after. They are variously described as muses, nymphs, Greek mythology-inspired characters and angels. When Tiffany & Co. in Hong Kong was commissioned to design new Lobby chinaware, they looked to the pillars and ceilings for inspiration. "But we could find no information, no references about the figures anywhere," said Tiffany's Wendy Hsu.

The Lobby was a difficult, frustrating and eminently satisfying challenge. Richmond's brief was to restore the room to its original classic beauty, without sacrificing any of its character. The job would require imported artisan's skills as well as incredible ingenuity in adding unobtrusive state-of-the-art technology, such as air-conditioning, electrical outlets embedded in the pillars and fire shutters. As with the rest of the original building, the Lobby had suffered the effects of, first, a lack of air-conditioning, and then from its imposition. For some time, the gold and white ceiling paint had been flaking so badly that netting had been placed over each bay, preventing unpalatable additions to teacups below and further dulling the once splendid effect. Although an initial assessment showed that most of the gargoyles topping the pillars, along with the cherubs and other figures on the ceilings and door arches, were badly damaged — some were completely saturated with water; others were so dried

Above, employing traditional techniques, a team of British craftsmen repaired the effects of time, heat and humidity, restoring the Lobby figures to pristine condition

out they were teetering on their perches — none were beyond repair.

By dint of its position and its popularity, the Lobby renovation wreaked terrific havoc. The room was restored one half at a time, beginning with the west side. In order to lay the limestone slabs in the centre of the floor, the main doors were closed and a wall was built along the carpet line. People reached the staircase, lifts and Reception via a tunnel that snaked through the construction site. "The only mistake we made was not putting in windows," said Mr. Hoffman, "because people would have loved to have been able to see what was going on."

Work on the ceiling was eventually to turn the room into a workplace that prompted inevitable comparisons to Michelangelo's Sistine Chapel labours. All the gold sections had to be sanded and repainted, and a team of British craftsmen were flown in to restore the plaster mouldings. Their painstaking task lasted seven months, much of it spent high up on platforms laid across Hong Kong's ubiquitous bamboo scaffolding, recreating and re-gilding the fine details of lavish geometric shapes, griffins, fronds and flowers and reconstructing the cherubs, nymphs and gargoyles on the ceiling and pillars.

The re-design of the ground floor meant some mouldings had to be sacrificed. But patterns were meticulously copied: grapes and partridges which border the original mirrors above the central steps were reproduced on the modern complementary mirrors. With the laying of a specially designed carpet, the staircase was once again a beautiful focal point. It is easy now to picture Mrs. Marjorie Angus on her wedding day in 1934: "When I was leaving I went and stood at the top of the main stairs and threw my bouquet — which was rather a long throw."

Above, restored Lobby cherub; *below*, The Peninsula Fu Dog takes pride of place in the Reception

Moving Reception to the tower area of the ground floor presented another challenge. "We wanted to have a sculpture," recalled Mr. Ronald McAulay, Chairman of the Arts Committee. "Through the Ho Gallery, we commissioned the Fu Dog from American sculptor Jim Dine." Majestic and endearing at the same time, the bronze creature is the perfect counterpoint to the old-world majesty of the Lobby. "In the same way that The Peninsula combines the modern and the traditional, the Fu Dog echoes the Chinese mythical animals at the door of the hotel, yet it is clearly a contemporary piece of art," said Mr. McAulay.

THE CHINA CLIPPER

As the China Clipper began to take unique shape on the 30th floor of the tower, contributions poured in from aviation enthusiasts who shared The Hon. Michael D. Kadoorie's passion for the golden age of flight. "Boxes of engine parts would land on my desk and the propeller arrived just eight months before the opening," recalled architect Darren Kindrachuk, of Hong Kong-based Denton, Corker, Marshall Interiors Ltd., who was entrusted with the design of this combination first-class helicopter arrival/departure area, exclusive venue for private functions and tribute to the pioneering spirit of the "flying boat" era.

Pan American Airways System pioneered the long-range ocean routes linking Asia and the United States, and commissioned the building of the Clipper flying boats which first delivered mail and then passengers on an island base-hopping journey. The first Clipper to land in Hong Kong was piloted by Pan American's president, Mr. Juan Trippe. Over 4,000 people watched the Martin M-130 skim to a landing in the harbour off Kai Tak on October 26, 1936. In a foreshadowing of the role the hotel was to play in aviation developments, Mr. Trippe, his passengers and crew stayed the night at The Peninsula.

The flight from California to Hong Kong took seven days then. But what the Clipper lacked in speed, it more than made up for in creature comforts. The M-130 offered passengers comfortable lounge chairs and settees, sleeping berths, a dining lounge and private dressing room. In *Wings Over Wake*, Dorothy Kaucher's account of her 1937 Clipper flight to Hong Kong, the author describes settling in for her first night on board: "I hoisted anchors away, me lads, and climbed in between two yellow sheets in the aft compartment. The steward said that yellow sheets would help passengers from getting airsick. Curtains were pulled around the separate berths. I asked him to call me for the sunrise. Clothes swayed smugly on coat hangers on the zippered wall. Then my backbone seemed to drop out as I buckled the strap over my chest."

The Clipper's aeronautical design aesthetics and superior cabin luxury became a model and inspiration for the modern-day lounge. The aviation theme is evoked as soon as one steps out of the private lift, with the window of an interior section of a DC-4 fuselage offering a

Far left, inspired by the adventurous era of the Clipper flying boats, the China Clipper is both modern lounge and aviation museum; *left*, a Pratt & Whitney radial engine from a DC-3, which was also used on flying boats

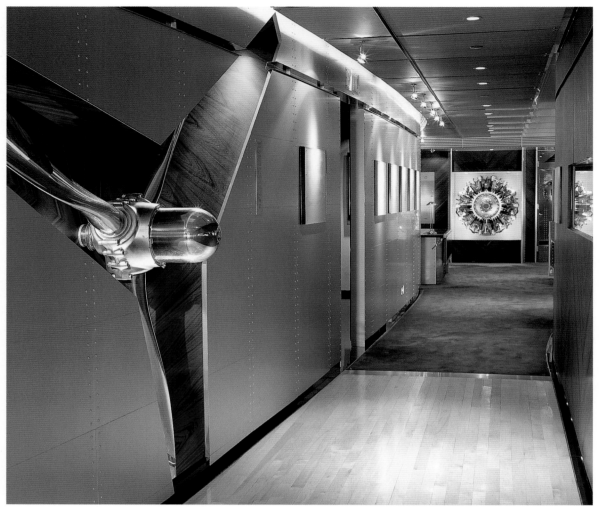

Preceding pages, the China Clipper doubles as an exclusive venue for intimate functions; *above*, a Hamilton Standard propeller; *right*, Kowloon-bound, aboard Heliservices' Aero-Spatiale AS355N Twin Squirrel; *far right*, one of the twin helipads that top the tower

vista over the eastern harbour. The entranceway which houses aviation artifacts is reminiscent of the mooring docks used by the flying boats. The main lounge echoes a cabin interior with its central aluminium vaulted ceiling, while rosewood panelling and aluminium cabinets create the atmosphere of an aviator's study. Rolex developed a special 24-hour movement for the world clocks set into the wall of the main area.

"It was all detail," said The Hon. Michael D. Kadoorie, who unapologetically described himself as "a tyrant in this respect" throughout the entire construction and renovation. "I threw out the screws in the China Clipper. The designers said, 'but they came from HAECO (Hong Kong Aircraft and Engineering Co.).' My response was, yes, but they're from jets; not

1940s propeller planes." Bruce Rabin co-ordinated the acquisition of machinery for the lounge; appropriately, a copy of *The Peddler In Paradise*, written by his father, Al Rabin, is in the display cabinet. Other aficionados contributed to the historical accuracy. The propeller embedded in the wall across from the display cabinets had three decals on it when it arrived. According to Mr. Kadoorie, "A gentleman who had worked at Hamilton Standard for years came to the lounge and said, 'Those aren't the right ones', and he gave us his own pre-war decals. The retired riveter who installed the aluminium dome head rivet fixings donated his rivet gun at the end of the job, in case we might need it later."

"There are three aircraft noted in the lounge: the Martin M-130 Clipper, which is the signature Clipper, the DC-3 and the Catalina flying boat, both of which were important in Hong Kong's aviation history," explained aviation expert Cliff Dunnaway, who worked closely

with The Hon. Michael D. Kadoorie and Mr. Kindrachuk, identifying the memorabilia. "One happy coincidence was that when I came to research the Pratt & Whitney engine, I suddenly noticed that this DC-3 engine we had was the one used in the Martin Clipper and the Catalina. So not only do we have a DC-3 engine, but we have an engine featured in the lounge that was used in all three planes. At first, I had thought it was a piece of oddball hardware."

From the pilot/helicopter operations area, one can watch airplanes coming in to land at Kai Tak Airport, their wheels seeming to almost brush the roofs of buildings lining the approach path. A communications link to the control tower — which also controls helicopter takeoffs and landings from The Peninsula tower — allows watchers to hear pilots and air traffic controllers as the craft dip out of sight, then appear moments later taxiing on the runway. When Chek Lap Kok Airport opens, the hotel's helicopters will make the journey from there to the hotel in about ten minutes. The China Clipper has been designed to provide for security and customs checks, baggage weighing and storage and to fulfil international passenger check-in requirements

Before the tower was completed, helicopter pilots flew their craft repeatedly past the structure for several days, conducting noise trials to reassure the Civil Aviation and Environmental authorities that there would not be undue disturbance.

Just six months before the official opening, the authorities insisted on having a barrier around the outside of the helipad to protect passengers in case of strong winds. John Simler, of Heliservices, came up with a retractable fence option, which proved acceptable. When a helicopter lands, the fence, which is connected by hydraulics to a control panel, is raised with the push of a button.

The harmony of historical and contemporary embodied in the China Clipper was evident at the official opening of the facility. Mr. Peter Lok, Hong Kong's Director of Civil Aviation, did the honours for the twin helipads, while Mr. Dick Smith, who completed the first round-the-world solo helicopter flight in 1983, and in 1985 the first circumnavigation of the globe in a Twin Otter aircraft, landing at both the North and South Poles, declared the China Clipper lounge open.

"The China Clipper continues The Peninsula's long association with civil aviation in Hong Kong, bringing new efficiency for our guests," said The Hon. Michael D. Kadoorie at the ceremony. "As we celebrate The Peninsula's new era, it is fitting that we should pay homage to one that is gone, but certainly not forgotten." Indeed, the China Clipper is playing an extremely important part in ensuring that the pioneering spirit and adventure of the "flying boat" era is truly celebrated.

ROOM SERVICE

When construction crews were still pouring concrete on the 19th floor of the tower, a fully functioning sample room on the 17th floor was undergoing close examination by a series of selected guests. One evening late in 1993, The Hon. Michael D. Kadoorie and his wife, Betty, stepped out of the exterior lift, hard hats in place, and followed the carefully laid ramps to room 1715. The next morning, their Room Service order was for "tea, coffee, yoghurt, Birchermüesli, five writing pads and six pencils". Based on the exacting couple's comments, chairs were redesigned, fax machines were set into desk drawers, reading lamps were made moveable and adjusted to offer two levels of brightness and drawers were added to the vanity table — and that was just page one!

Before Room 1715 even existed, its forerunner had taken up brief residence amid the pre-demolition chaos on the fifth floor of the original building. Consisting of a plywood shell furnished with plywood mock-ups built to the interior designers' specifications, the unprepossessing debut guest room was an important part of a process employed on every one of The Hongkong and Shanghai Hotels, Limited's projects.

"Our brief was to create the room of a westerner who had travelled extensively in the Far East," said Ray Greenfield, then project manager for Richmond International.

After the mock-up room came the model room, which incorporated changes made in response to the mock-up and which featured all the proposed finishes, carpets, electrical provisions, furniture and architectural and free-

Far left, and left, numerous refinements to the mock-up room led to the perfectly-tuned comfort, space and grace of the guest rooms

standing lights. "It was like a film set," marvelled Greenfield. This, too, went through several finely-tuned evolutions. The inset line within the floral line on the bathroom floors was changed from two inches to three inches wide, for instance. The mood light settings in the bathrooms are the result of Mr. Kadoorie's insistence on getting it absolutely right. He personally set the mood lighting levels by sitting in a bathtub from sunset till midnight. "When I found that we couldn't get uniform light levels on the floor master control," he said, "we bought a HK$5,000 light meter and we used it to set the proper standards."

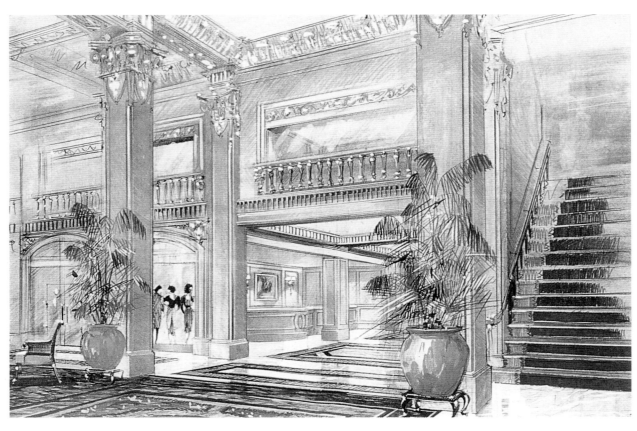

Above, artist's conception of the Lobby; *below*, marble floor tile; *below right*, the Lobby under renovation; *far right*, the completed suite

When the model room had finally met with management's satisfaction, the coterie of contractors and designers was charged with building production samples based on the model room, with every element, from lamps to chairs to tables to sinks, meeting the standards achieved in the model. The result was room 1715.

Along with official testing by group staff, some of The Peninsula's regular guests were invited to don hard hats and travel via an exterior lift to spend a night in the very first tower room. A command post was organised, with a fireman, an engineer and a security guard keeping watch, while friends of The Pen sampled and critiqued a preview of what was to come.

In true "nothing is left to chance" spirit, mock-ups of a lift car and a Lobby shop façade were created. The lift replica was built adjacent to the mock-up room and featured the entire proposed interior, right down to the call buttons. The shop mock-up was a different case altogether. By the 1990s, the Davidoff shop was the last example of a 20-year-old style; the question was whether to reinstate that look or compose an entirely new one for all the Lobby boutiques. The then Design Manager, Paul Sheppard, and his team built a secondary old-style shopfront in front of one of the boutiques at the opposite end to the original. "The Lobby is almost a hall of mirrors, so you could see what it would look like if all the shopfronts were returned to the old style," said Sheppard. The decision was unanimously in favour of reverting to what is familiarly called the "Davidoff style".

By the time the extension programme began, the staff facilities on the roof of the original building had become outdated and uncomfortable. During typhoon season, the thundering tattoo of heavy rain on the staff canteen's corrugated tin roof was enough to drown out even the liveliest extremes of Cantonese conversation. Changing rooms had expanded beyond the confines of four walls, which wasn't a problem until The Kowloon Hotel was built, directly overlooking The Peninsula, roof and all. Comments from guests in the neighbouring hotel, whose harbour view gave them more than they had bargained for, urged more rooftop discretion. The announcement that the dilapidated staff eyrie was to be replaced with fully equipped changing rooms and a comfortable restaurant within the new back-of-house area was welcome news. To everyone, that is, except for the dozen or so men who not only worked at The Peninsula, but who called it home, as well.

English classes help page boys build a career with The Pen

"I started at The Peninsula 38 years ago as an office boy, delivering messages."

Johnny Chung Kam-hung is a dapper man with a glorious smile. In 1988, a local magazine pronounced his dry martinis the best in town and put the barman with the infectious grin on the cover. Inside was a report on his winning technique. "Beefeater gin, Noilly Prat vermouth, no measures used. On the rocks or straight up. The ingredients were mixed in a pouring sifter and served in cocktail glasses, with the lemon wiped around the rim and dropped in. Judgment: A perfect, dry Martini."

"My father worked here as a Lobby Captain. I used to visit him and I

Evenings in the Bar are
lively and intimate

hoped I would be able to work in such a grand place." That day came sooner than

he would have wished when his father passed away and 13-year-old Johnny Chung

came to work at the hotel. "After I was an office boy, I became a bar coolie — that's

the old name," he said. "Every morning, I took water, coconut water, soda and tonic

to the Lobby Bar." Now Senior Barman in the Service Kitchen, he has poured drinks

in the Moorish Bar, L'Apéritif, the Verandah Lounge and The Bar. William Holden,

he will tell you, liked scotch and water served English-style, with one ice cube.

Chung has lived at The Peninsula since he joined the hotel. "On the roof

it was very hot in summer, because there was no air conditioning." During the 1970s

and 1980s, the staff quarters gradually emptied. One's place of work no longer dictated

one's place of residence, and as the economy improved, people purchased flats and

wanted to spend more time with their families. By 1990, only a handful of older

bachelors retired to the roof at the end of their shift. When the directors learned

that the extension would effectively put a dozen staff out of house and home, they

instructed that provision be made for these men within the new back-of-house area. While construction was underway, Johnny Chung and his colleagues moved next door to the YWCA for six weeks. When they returned to the hotel, it was to a spacious, air-conditioned dormitory.

"The bottom line dictates these days, but somehow the Kadoories have managed to insinuate compassion and so staff stayed and stayed," said Priscilla Chen, former Public Relations Manager. "By the time I worked there, in the early 1980s, I was meeting third generation staff. In a city where permanence was always slightly in question, I found permanence at The Peninsula."

B y the middle of 1994, the seemingly never-ending story was nearing its conclusion. The designers contracted for the renovation of the existing hotel had embarked upon their various tasks the previous autumn and the west wing of rooms was almost completed. The jackhammers had long since ceased their daily mind-numbing din; instead, the harsh staccato of drills and hammers assaulted the air as battalions of workmen laid carpets, painted walls and ceilings, installed light fixtures and moved furniture. From this chaotic scene emerged the gracious, elegant rooms of the tower, at a rate of one floor every seven to ten days. By the time the scaffolding and temporary works — the last vestiges of the project — came down, it was the autumn of 1995, a little more than five years after the physical works had begun and nearly a decade since its inception.

BATHED IN LUXURY

Carved sycamore doors frame a vision in blue and white bounded by a soothing waterfall and a wide, marbled sun terrace. From this tranquil vantage point, Hong Kong is an appealing backdrop, its hectic pulse muted by an ambience of cool peace. The uninhibited serenity of The Peninsula's swimming pool is the brainchild of Cuban-born, San Francisco-based designer Orlando Diaz-Azcuy. His disarming lack of pretension, blended with exquisite taste and a seemingly innate talent for creating subtle effect have shaped a refuge which, as he intended, "transports you into a romantic place".

Eschewing the popular tendency toward Roman-Grecian baths, Diaz-Azcuy plays with

Pure indulgence; absolute relaxation

elements of that theme, while imposing a stronger personality that throws contrasting elements into sharp relief. "The four columns that support the tower are in this space," he explained. "Two go right through the pool and the others are inside the volumes on either side of the cascade. The columns are six feet in diameter, so of course there's no way we can hide them — let's not be pretentious about it!" The interference gave Diaz-Azcuy inspiration. "Let's take the idea that you are transported to this other world. You see the sky. The friezes on the columns are so over-scaled, you feel like a little fish. You're almost swimming in the sky." The designer took a tongue-in-cheek approach to the friezes, deliberately leaving them incomplete. "I did not want to create a set for a movie."

Nor did he wish to forsake the urban surroundings and create a *faux* resort oasis. This swimming pool is not an idiosyncratic diversion, it is emphatically of The Peninsula. Diaz-Azcuy borrowed from the Lobby, copying the muses on the ceiling onto the great sycamore doors. The pool's deep blue tiles bordered by triangular gold details on the perimeter, the light fixtures finished in gold leaf, all resonate with the richness of the hotel. The colonnade around the pool repeats the Lobby's nymph theme. "I wanted to bring elements of that into the pool area, so that you would have the sense that the pool could only happen at The Peninsula."

Designer Orlando Diaz-Azcuy blended an innate sense of whimsy with Peninsula-inspired motifs

Individual, yet cohesive; the Hong Kong Institute of Architects awarded its highest honour to The Peninsula extension

"A remarkable achievement", both technically and aesthetically, pronounced the Hong Kong Institute of Architects in March, 1996. In granting Rocco Design their top prestigious Silver Award, the judges of the Society's awards committee praised The Peninsula tower's "architectural language"; in their considered opinion, the structure succeeded in blending well with the existing building, while asserting its own identity.

The approbation was a much-deserved tribute to Rocco Yim's work on a project that had taxed his technical and creative skills. "There are so many aspects to it that are really not standardised construction, they're more like product design," he said, such as in interpreting the concepts visualised by Orlando Diaz-Azcuy. Yim's team made two models of the unique floor-to-ceiling retractable glass wall that surrounds the pool area. The Chairman's requirement was that the glass panels be suspended, to eliminate the need for floor grooves which could catch the feet of unwary bathers. With the model approved, then came an exhaustive search for a manufacturer who could produce the unusual glass wall. Eventually, Gartner in Berlin took on the job.

THE LOGISTICS OF DRAMA

For all that The Peninsula is Hong Kong's Grand Old Lady, when it comes to technology, she's a child of the future. The six engineers and more than 20 technicians in the group's dedicated technology unit not only reshape and retool existing hardware, they develop the software for advanced systems that have leaders of international communications networks shaking their heads in amazement.

Soundless fax machines that signal receipt of a communication via a light at the entrance to the guest's room and on the bedside panel, and telephones with touch panels programmed for instant connection to restaurants are examples of how the technology team take an existing product, consider how guests should be able to use it and alter it accordingly. Among their innovations is a remote control that speaks to every piece of the entertainment console, switching from satellite television to the laser disc player to the compact disc player with the push of a button. A useful panel beside the door of each room and suite indicates whether there are any messages, and displays the temperature outdoors (in fahrenheit and celsius) and the humidity level.

Simplicity and logic govern every aspect of the technology designed for guest rooms

"Mood lighting" communicates a sense of drama

"We had three things to consider," said Fraser Hickox, the group's Research and Technology Manager. "One was the communications aspect; the second was that everything had to be logical; and the third was that this is a five-star hotel, so there should be a bit of a show."

Each room is equipped with two-line telephones designed to incorporate the potential introduction of ISDN communications systems and the much-vaunted video telephone. At The Pen, guests can hold a dignified business conversation while sitting in the bath and watching television. The three hands-free telephones have been digitally filtered so that neither the usual cavernous sound or the noise of running bath water can be heard by the caller, and the volume on the radio and television dips automatically when the telephone rings and returns to normal level when the call is finished.

As much as the provision of this sophisticated technology, it is the frustration-free ease of operation which guests appreciate. The bedside panel alone is a masterpiece of logic. Along with operating the lights, the bedroom entertainment console and the curtains, guests can mute the telephone with the press of a "Do Not Disturb" button. Headphone jacks allow guests to use their personal sound systems or watch television without disturbing their partner. When the lights go off, the lighting in the panel dims; the proximity detector in the panel causes it to brighten when a hand is reached out toward it. The "night light" switch turns on the bathroom light and gently illuminates the path there.

The theatrics are most apparent in the lighting: the bathroom has a three-setting mood illumination and the reading lights over the bed dim slowly when the master lights are switched off. "The technology in The Peninsula evolved as the building was built and it's still evolving," said Hickox. "Since it's a software structure we have the ability to continually change it." The electronics panels are located outside the rooms, in a black box set into the hallway, so that alterations and repairs can be made without repairmen even entering the room.

In 1992, the Group integrated a PC-LAN (local area network) system to handle reservations, accounting, sales, marketing and group event management. The new system also swept away the old practice of laboriously recording guest histories on cards. Existing information was entered into the database, and since then guests will return to The Peninsula and find that the extra pillows have already been provided, that their welcome tea is served without fuss when their baggage is delivered, that their usual lunch time table at the Verandah has been reserved.

Developments on the horizon include the installation of a new technology incorporating ADSI, which the Group is working on with Bell and Northern Telecom, to allow guests to collect and transmit e-mail without their computers. The next logical step will be enabling computer-free guests to browse the Internet. Televisions and remote controls have already been adapted to handle three-digit channels. "The next generation of telephones will offer a facility whereby you are able to have a conversation with someone and see them," says Hickox. "We've already written the software to support that." Another forthcoming innovation is the "smart card" which will carry a guest's history with the group, thus facilitating quicker check-in.

The smart card will enable guests to store an infinite number of frequently dialled telephone numbers — and arrange them so that the first numbers correspond to the city in which the caller finds him- or herself.

"It's not technology for the sake of having all the bells and whistles, it's technology that's useful," stressed Hickox. Which explains why the old-fashioned shoebox, a feature of guest rooms since the hotel opened, was built into every tower room. People have always appreciated being able to simply put their shoes inside the box and press the Valet button to alert the room attendant to the fact that there are shoes to shine. At 4 am, or thereabouts, he or she will silently replace the shoes, alongside the daily newspaper. It is not fancy; it is simple and effective and it shares those qualities with every other piece of technology in the rooms.

Observing the conventions: the shoebox has been a feature of guest rooms since The Peninsula opened

Windows turned out to be the cause of much mind-bending creativity. Eighteen models were produced of the new façade in the quest to ensure that it would blend with the old. Since six floors in the old building equalled eight in the new, spandrels were designed to give the tower windows the illusion of looking bigger. When a manufacturer could not be found to prefabricate the massive double-glazed window required for Felix, on the basis that the dimensions were simply too large for their factories to manage, the architects installed the parallel window on site.

Above, His Royal Highness The Duke of Kent raises a glass with The Hon. Michael D. Kadoorie at the grand opening of The Peninsula tower; *below*, Their Royal Highnesses The Duke and The Duchess of Kent, The Hon. Mr. and Mrs. Michael D. Kadoorie and Chan Pak are surrounded by page boy-costumed children, one for each year of The Pen's existence

For The Hongkong and Shanghai Hotels, Limited, this marked the third occasion on which their projects had been singled out by the Hong Kong Institute of Architects. Silver Awards, the Society's top honour, had been bestowed on the architects responsible for the redevelopment of the company's St. John's Building and The Repulse Bay complex.

The Hon. Mr. and Mrs.
Michael D. Kadoorie
dance to the exuberant
strains of a mariachi band

With a flourish of velvet curtains, His Royal Highness The Duke of Kent unveiled a plaque to commemorate the grand opening of The Peninsula tower and, with The Hon. Michael D. Kadoorie, raised a glass of champagne to the assembled crowd. It was December 1, 1994, and before the day was through, many special ceremonies would be observed, literally thousands of champagne corks would pop and recognition would be made of the staff and guests whose support of The Peninsula had contributed so much to this occasion. In addition, Mr. Kadoorie paid moving tribute to his late father, Lord Kadoorie, and to his uncle, Sir Horace.

"Each department sent two or three representatives to the grand opening party, to the Lobby, to greet the royal guests," said Peter Borer. "So there was a kitchen steward in his Wellingtons next to the Duchess of Kent. The Peninsula was dancing faster than she ever had, and that's what we really wanted."

Almost a decade after it was conceived, The Peninsula tower stood proud and tall above Kowloon. The hotel was, at last, as The Hon. Michael D. Kadoorie, Chairman of The Hongkong and Shanghai Hotels, Limited, said, "ready to greet the new century with pride and confidence".

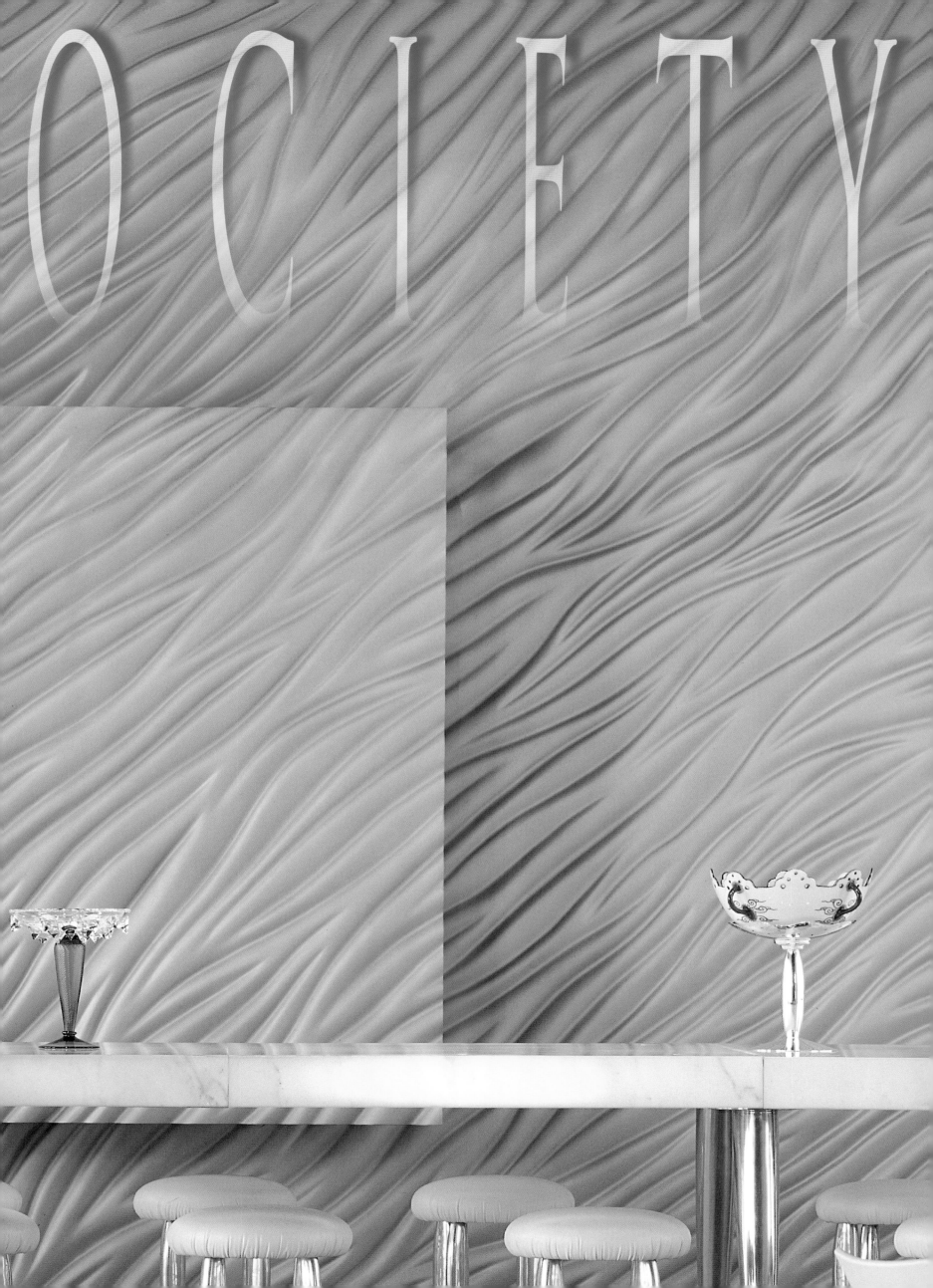

HIGH SOCIETY

ext to a table heaped high with a froth of ferns, baskets that look like they've been fashioned from a thinly-sliced section of peat moss and tightly rolled twists of the twine used by bamboo scaffolders to secure their framework sits the head florist, gently blowing air into a tightly budded red rose. "The client asked for roses that are open," she said. It will take 20 to 30 minutes to coax the dozens of flowers into the desired fullness before they can

Preceding pages, the wave of the future: aluminium relief wall in Felix; *left*, the Salisbury Room; *below*, birthday festivities at The Pen

be wound around the massive, ornate Christofle candelabras that will grace the tables for an anniversary party in the Salisbury Room. People are particular about roses. The flower room staff loves to tell the story about the guest who asked for rose petals sprinkled on his bed — in the shape of a heart.

The Pen has always loved a party. In the early days, when Hong Kong deserved its reputation as a colonial backwater, the rich and bored were attracted to its never-ending medley of balls, dances, teas and recitals like bees to honey. "To those who find it a job to amuse themselves on Sundays we highly recommend a visit to The Peninsula Lounge, where we are sure that they will find the finest entertainment obtainable in the Territory of a Sunday evening," promised *Tavern Topics* in June, 1932, announcing a weekly symphony concert, effective immediately.

Not even the installation of ping pong tables ("Ping pong is played a great deal in England and America and there is no reason why it should not be popular in Hong Kong") could console the magazine's editor the following month: "With the flight of many of our friends to cooler climes, including the Navy's summer visit to Weiheiwei, the colony seems to be quite deserted; indeed, July and August are very appropriately described as dog days for Hong Kong." Only the prospect of autumn and looking ahead to "the annual visits of some of the large tourist liners, to tennis and cricket and football to provide us with something more exciting to talk about" allowed the *Timely Topics* page to end on a slightly upbeat note.

"Dog days" aside, Hong Kong welcomed any excuse for a gala. The Peninsula put on breathtaking Christmas and New Year programmes of dinner dances and buffet lunches. Invitations to the annual fête of the Royal Hong Kong Yacht Club, the Fanling Hunt Club, the Hong Kong Automobile Association and the Society for the Prevention of Cruelty to Animals, among others, directed guests to cross the harbour to Kowloon. People flocked to St. Patrick's nights, Chinese New Year carnivals, balls and galas for just about any occasion. On Empire Day in 1933, The Peninsula presented European meals on the first floor and a cold buffet in the Dining Room and reactivated the "emergency bar — which proved so handy to many a fainting soul last year". Tea dances, held daily except Sunday from 4:30 pm to 6:30 pm in the Rose Room, were "constantly filled to overflowing, being the scene of Hong Kong's daily fashion parade".

It was the pomp and ceremony of the grand balls which put The Peninsula on the society map. In 1929, the St. Andrew's Society broke a tradition of nearly 50 years and abandoned City Hall in favour of the Kowloon hostelry. The Roof Garden Ballroom had not exactly been languishing, but this seal of approval opened the social floodgates. The band played on throughout the 1930s, right up to the eve of the Japanese invasion, when 800 people attended the Hong Kong Chinese Women's Club Fancy Dress Victory Ball on December 7, 1941.

After the war, when the Rose Room had been converted first to dormitories, then guest rooms, the balls resembled dignified games of musical chairs: cocktails were sipped upstairs in the Verandah, dinner was served by white-gloved waiters in the Lobby ("People smoked after the meal," said three-time General Manager Felix Bieger. "You couldn't see from one side of the Lobby to the other."), then it was back up to the first floor for dancing. Mrs. Hazel Javier, who in 1963 was Manageress of the Cake Shop and then transferred to Room Service, recalled "flowers galore". Mrs. Javier's household had reason to eagerly anticipate these occasions. "Just before my shift ended at 10 pm, my good friend, the waiter Ah Woo, surprised me with a large newspaper parcel," she said. "He had collected almost ten pounds of leftovers for my two dogs." Her pets loved haggis left over from the St. Andrew's Ball as much as they did the more usual roast beef and spare ribs.

These nights of extravagance dwindled in frequency in the late 1960s and throughout the 1970s and in January 1978, the Ballroom was closed, renovated and re-opened as Gaddi's. The Peninsula still provided many a reason for ball gown and dinner jacket to be donned. Small wedding receptions, corporate functions, anniversaries and other gatherings proliferated in the function rooms, while the annual New Year's Day morning Egg-Nog Party in the Lobby became the season's most popular occasion. Former General Manager Urs Aeby chose the 1984 gathering to spring a carefully-planned surprise. He arranged for Colin Wood, leader of the Royal Hong Kong Police Band, traditional music-meisters for this event, to invite Canadian journalist Katie Keeley to conduct a song. When the last notes died out, the bandmaster presented Ms. Keeley with a small package and insisted she open it then and there. Inside was an engagement ring, which Urs placed on her finger.

The question had been popped the night before, "in true general manager style", laughed Mrs. Aeby, more than 12 years and two children later. "We drove up to the Peak. Urs had brought along a picnic basket with champagne, chilled glasses — three, in case one broke — and two cameras, in case one didn't work." The couple had met at The Peninsula four months before, when Ms. Keeley arrived to shoot a number of television interviews, despite Mr. Aeby having several times turned down her persistent requests for a complimentary room. He finally changed his mind…and his life.

——◆━◆━◆——

"At Gaddi's, everything is perfection and it's very, very rewarding." Now in his 30th year as maître d'hôtel of Hong Kong's premier restaurant, Rolf Heiniger is intimately acquainted with the demands of instilling and maintaining perfection. "When I arrived in 1966, meats were frozen and everything came by ship," he said. "Then, we had an extra Indian cook who would make curries for the local residents. Now, there are no seasons; we can get what we want from various places at different times, and our chef is always French." In its earliest days, Gaddi's menu was a far cry from the purely French fare that is its signature today. Then, chefs cooked Russian and Chinese dishes for patrons, and in 1954 a team from the restaurant won a major Swiss cooking competition with a Chinese dish: sweet and sour pork.

The opening of Gaddi's, in December 1953, was the first expression of The Peninsula's ambition to define and interpret a distinctive dining experience. Hong Kong people, and the growing numbers of visitors attracted to the Territory by business or travel, were more worldly, and such institutions as the Dining Room had become outmoded. Horace Kadoorie, then Chairman of The Hongkong and Shanghai Hotels, Limited, recognised that instilling personality was as important as achieving high standards of service and cuisine, and dubbed it "Gaddi's", after the hotel's illustrious manager and recognised personality, Leo Gaddi. Sir Horace's intention was as much to ensure Leo Gaddi's complete dedication to what was a risky venture — the creation of a fine dining experience in a city still suffering post-war privations. As with any of the hotel projects, Sir Horace involved himself in every element of the new venture: he and Leo Gaddi toured Europe's finest five-star restaurants to assess standards and styles of service and cuisine; he appropriated Gaddi's distinctive signature for the logo, designed the menus and fixed on the red-and-gold decor in a glorious celebration of the coronation of Queen Elizabeth II.

Left, not only was the restaurant named for him, Leo Gaddi's distinctive signature became its logo; *below,* antique duck press on display in Gaddi's

Tino Yung Pak Chuen was promoted to Head Waiter in Gaddi's in 1980, when the venerable Chan Pak semi-retired and moved to the Catering Department. "When I started in the Verandah in 1961, there were so many levels of apprenticeship," he said. "It would take a few promotions to move up to Waiter. I started as a Junior Waiter in Gaddi's in 1962, counting linen and cleaning silverware. Gaddi's was on the ground floor — I'd count the linen, make a list, put it all in a big bag, put the bag over my shoulder and take it up the stairs. So heavy!"

Yung quickly ascended the complex hierarchy, moving from Junior Waiter to Waiter to Chef du Roux, Wine Waiter, Junior Captain, Captain, Assistant Head Waiter and, finally, Head Waiter. "I was promoted very fast; I was quite young compared to other staff. And I learned very fast, I could speak some English." It was his facility with English that had led Tsui Tim, comprador of The Peninsula, to hire him. "My father's friend got me an interview with Tsui Tim," recalled Yung. "He gave me a book in English

and asked me to read to him. It was the first time I had read out loud to someone. I was so nervous! Fortunately, he was satisfied." Tsui Tim's beaming face can be seen in the pictures of Pen staff taken on opening day. As comprador (generally, the agent for a foreign-run business), he had complete responsibility for and control over anything having to do with food and beverage. He purchased all the food and wine, hired and fired restaurant and stewarding staff and managed all the restaurant outlets. Though they thought the situation unusual, each new Swiss chef and manager accepted the status quo.

Preceding pages, splendour and intimacy harmonise in Gaddi's private room; *above,* Gaddi's Supper Club, 1971

Gaddi's has moved three times: from the first to the ground floor and back again to the first floor, to occupy the former ballroom space. In the late 1960s, the red carpet and red velvet chairs were replaced by champagne-coloured walls, rust velvet chairs and gold carpet. The three-tiered room included a dance floor on the lowest level. In 1994, the restaurant opened after a hiatus of eight months, this time elegantly draped in subtle shades of beige, cream and gold. In all its incarnations, the one constant has been the priceless 17th century Coromandel screen depicting the Emperor K'ang Hsi and his consort in the Summer Palace. The magnificent work of art was loaned to the restaurant by the late Lord Kadoorie and is one of a pair made in 1690 by Fong Long Kon for the Imperial Palace in Beijing. The second screen was donated to the Metropolitan Museum of Art in New York by J. Pierpont Morgan in 1906.

"I had a table of eight at the latest reopening," recalled long-time patron, Stan Freedman. "Rolf knew I also spent time in another hotel restaurant and when the menus were brought to the table, everyone received a Gaddi's menu, but Rolf presented me with one from that other restaurant."

Jack Ormut, Chairman of Manchu Inc., has eaten countless meals at Gaddi's and he has one of the restaurant's older menus at his home in Toronto to prove it. "A friend of mine brought that menu to The Peninsula, sat at a table in Gaddi's, opened it up and argued with Rolf about the prices." Waving away the contemporary *carte*, Mr. Ormut said to the waiter, "Rolf knows what I want." It is that awareness of individuals that distinguishes Gaddi's. As the impeccably dressed maître d'hôtel wheels over a trolley, gently clinking with bottles of oil and vinegar and herbs, Mr. Ormut confides to his companions that nowhere has he found a Caesar Salad to rival Rolf's.

Even this rarefied atmosphere has seen its share of unusual, if not downright eccentric, customers. "There was a Greek gentleman who would eat in Gaddi's and break the dishes across his knee at the end of the meal," recalled The Hon. Michael D. Kadoorie. "The management, conscious of the cost of this activity and the need to preserve the expensive dinnerware, gave him old plates and charged him for the ones he broke. He was quite happy to pay!" Another gentleman once asked the waiter what the specialties were and then ordered the lot of them. "He ate them all, too," said Mr. Kadoorie. "He was in the restaurant until 4 pm."

Very soon after opening in 1953, Gaddi's was renowned well beyond Hong Kong as one of the finest restaurants east of Suez. Granted, there was little enough competition at the time, but it is telling to note that Gaddi's has retained its superiority, seeing off its many rivals throughout the years and sailing through the trend away from grill rooms and fine dining. A glance around the dinner crowd shows that the young and cultured are as enamoured of the experience as those patrons who can recall the second, or even the first, Gaddi's.

—◆◆◆—

For certain Felix guests, restaurant manager Cindy Lam and her staff pull out the booklet which gives the name and occupation of the people whose faces gaze out from the chairs in the main room. They answer detailed questions about

the chinaware and conduct carefully timed tours of the infamous men's toilet, with its marble urinals set against a floor-to-ceiling window overlooking Kowloon. In short, they do all they can to satiate the burning curiosity of the self-styled Philippe Starck fans who fly in from Japan, North America and Europe to experience how this much talked about collection of thematic expressions actually feels and functions.

Conversant with Starck's body of work, which ranges from lemon-squeezers to an Olympic torch to restaurants and hotels, they assess the use of the Royalton Stool (from Starck's renovation of the Royalton Hotel in New York) around the Long Table and try out what is now known in the Starck lexicon as The Peninsula Chair. Generally architects or interior designers, they ask, "Did he design the chinaware?" "The glassware?" (yes to both questions). The staff affectionately call these fans "Philippe Starck junkies".

If Gaddi's is firmly anchored in the traditional, Felix is its polar opposite. The designer most often described as "eclectic" was given a brief to create "a brasserie for the 21st century". Starck let loose an avant-garde vision in which divergent themes are intriguingly juxtaposed. From high up in the American Bar, the full impact of the combination of different environments can be appreciated. The main restaurant is flanked by two "snails" — bucket-shaped areas wrapped around illuminated spiral staircases, which contain the Balcony, the Wine Bar, the Crazy Box mini-discotheque and the American Bar. An incredible kaleidoscope of textures and materials has been applied to Felix's surfaces: mahogany walls meet aluminium reliefs in an almost audible jolt; there are marble tables in the restaurant, wooden tables in the wine bar, crystal stools around the dance floor, while the raised Long Table, stretching across the width of the main restaurant, is of ivory onyx gently lit by soft interior lights.

Left, in Felix, Philippe Starck devised a cocktail of the whimsical and the avant-garde; *above*, salt and pepper shakers

"Felix is fun and it's a challenge." Chef Bryan Nagao, who worked most recently at Roy Yamaguchi's famous eponymous restaurants in Hawaii, revels in the freedom he's been given to tempt palates with his own particular style of Pacific Rim cuisine. "I define it as ingredients and styles of cooking from areas that touch the Pacific," he explained. "There are influences from Thailand, Japan and China, with Californian techniques of presentation and sauces and Hawaiian ingredients."

Above, from the toothpick holder to the oil and vinegar bottles *(below),* Felix's every detail reflects the inspired vision behind the restaurant's inception

Hence, dishes like Citrus-Miso Seared Wild Salmon and Coconut-Macadamia Nut Prawn Sticks.

A group of architecture students sip their cappuccinos at the Long Table and discuss the way in which the aluminium "wave wall" behind the Long Table sets the main theme, which is carried through in the tableware, the lifts and the entranceway. "I love the way the dip in the lift lights and the darkness of the entrance suspends the drama," says one. "Felix works well — logistically and dramatically."

The stunning double-glazed window is the best example of this harmony. Specially designed fans placed between the two gigantic walls of glass prevent condensation from marring the spectacular view. Wooden blinds allow the eye to take in the view, without being completely overwhelmed.

Not everyone was convinced that The Peninsula needed a rooftop restaurant. "The hotel operators didn't want it," said The Hon. Michael D. Kadoorie bluntly. "I visited a restaurant in Madrid,

called Teatriz, that Starck had done and immediately thought this might be something for us." Despite having announced that he would undertake no further design projects, Starck was intrigued by Mr. Kadoorie's proposal and agreed to make a presentation to the board of The Hongkong and Shanghai Hotels, Limited. "I knew Starck would be a shock, but I was sure he would win the day without any undue influence from me," said Mr. Kadoorie. "I thus made sure I was out of Hong Kong when he met our executive board and five minutes into his meeting, they bought it lock, stock and barrel."

"Next, the hoteliers had to be won over," said Mr. Kadoorie. "I took Felix Bieger and Onno Poortier up in a helicopter, flew across the harbour and adjacent to the level where Felix would be situated in the soon-to-be-built tower, turned the helicopter around and said, 'There, that's your view'. They changed their minds and we had our restaurant."

━━•◆•◆•━━

The Verandah has had a chequered past. It has adopted and cast off different personas, changing names, menus and ambience. Yet despite this apparently fickle nature, it has remained the favourite restaurant of countless guests and local residents. Before the controversial contours of the Hong Kong Cultural Centre interfered with the view, people gathered on the Verandah to enjoy the tableau of ships gliding against the backdrop of the Peak, or to enjoy the colourful waterplay of the fountain in the hotel's forecourt.

In one of the earliest photographs of The Peninsula, taken in 1927, soldiers quartered in the unfinished, and unopened, hotel stand in orderly formation on the open verandah. While waiting for a call to protect British interests in Shanghai that never came, the 2nd Battalion Coldstream Guards and a battalion of the Devonshire Regiment held military drills daily along Salisbury Road.

Several years later, in 1933, *Tavern Topics* reported that: "The new canopy over the first floor verandah is now completed. With the warmer weather to come, we look to find this cool situation for the 'sundowner' more and more appreciated." During the grandest of balls, the partition between the Ballroom and verandah would be removed, and the carpets taken up to make an even grander dance floor. Appreciation of this space grew so much, not only for cocktails but for meals too, that in 1950, the verandah was enclosed and briefly called "the Playpen". Happily, that undignified name didn't last long and The Pen's newest restaurant soon became known simply

as the Verandah. Guest Joseph Stuart Sykes wrote of the pre-enclosed location: "I think one of the most delightful aspects of staying at The Pen in those days was coming down to breakfast on the Verandah, then open to the elements. "The elements" in those days was usually a nice, soft, early morning breeze off the harbour,

Preceding pages, afternoon tea in the Verandah is a soothing affair; *above,* after the Verandah was enclosed in 1950, the restaurant underwent several transformations. In the late 1960s, French food and formality prevailed

and there was always a mango and a kipper for breakfast."

The mango and kipper breakfast went the way of the Playpen. By 1965, advertisements invited the public to enjoy "European and Chinese food served in this portico style restaurant which overlooks the harbour and Hong Kong's famous Peak. Open for breakfast, lunch and dinner, serving à la carte or table d'hôte." French cuisine belonged to Gaddi's, but the Verandah menu was not without its soupçon of Gallic flavour, offering "Salade Caesar pour deux $30" and "Soupe à la Tortue (Turtle) Lady Curzon $12".

"The Verandah is my favourite restaurant in the world," said Mrs. Trust.

She and her husband have been staying at The Pen since 1962. In the mid-1970s, the couple brought their young children to Hong Kong for the first time. "It was the Christmas holidays. On New Year's Eve, every restaurant in the hotel was closed because they were preparing for all the special functions. There was nowhere for the kids to have dinner, so they opened up the Verandah just for them." Further along is the large circular table which staff know to reserve for the Trusts' daily business meetings during their bi-annual trips to Hong Kong.

Lam Siu Ping began working at The Pen in 1976, as a busboy attending three mealtime shifts a day in the Verandah. "There were yellow tablecloths, the room was very open and outside the windows there was nothing — just the view," he said. Later that year, the restaurant underwent another metamorphosis, emerging as the Verandah Grill.

"At that time, we did a lot of gueridon service; the Captains would make black pepper steak, flambé dishes, slice chicken and duck and make Crêpes Suzette." Moky Lam now manages the restaurant in which he began his career in 1986. "Standards were — and still are — very strict," he said. "Then, the coffee cup handle had to be at a 90 degree angle to the saucer, with the spoon parallel to the handle." Regular training sessions addressed the still prevalent lack of awareness of western food. "We would learn what cheese is, how and when it's served," recalled Mr. Lam. These days, the bi-monthly classes reflect the greater knowledge shared by staff, focusing on wine varietals and subtleties in spices and sauce preparation.

The 1990s renovation returned a pleasing measure of old-style grace to the Verandah, restoring the fans which used to soothe the diners of the 1950s. The dress code has relaxed somewhat, as has the ambience, "But we still have a certain standard," said Mr. Lam.

One of the most endearing qualities of The Peninsula is the genuine willingness to please the customer. The Verandah menu is a classic example. As tastes evolved, and trends changed, dishes which had gone out of vogue were dropped, only to be reinstated when customers voiced their disapproval. A late-1980s Winter Menu from the Verandah Grill gives a hint of this accommodation with Supreme of Chicken Lady Astor and Lobster Playpen (the original recipe) listed among "The Peninsula Favourites". That category still graces the current menu, offering Prawns Piri-Piri, Veal Steak Peninsula and Garoupa Shashlik. And when regular customer Jack Ormut, who prefers the Verandah's lunchtime ambience but Gaddi's Caesar Salad, if you will, and tossed by Jack, please, Gaddi's Captain thinks nothing of coming from the French restaurant to preside over the neighbouring restaurant's gueridon to prepare the salad and present it to Mr. Ormut.

—■—◆—◆—■—

Nestled within Chesa's cosy embrace, surrounded by walls of dark wood panelling and white stucco under a canopy of knotted-pine beams, it takes but a short flight of fancy to imagine that beyond the *faux* window frames blows a gusty winter wind, thick with snow. For Chesa is one of those rarities of hotel restaurants, presenting an environment so strikingly distinct and finely tuned that venturing past its heavy carved door, one enters a tiny, rustic pocket of Switzerland. Sipping on a thick brew of Schoppa de Giuotto, the traditional Swiss barley cream soup, then dipping hefty cubes of bread into a cheese fondue of Gruyère and Emmenthal cheeses laced with champagne and dill, the illusion is infused into all five senses.

It used to be the Bamboo Bar, just a swizzle stick's throw from the Reading Room. But when, in 1963, a Swiss food promotion, called "Rathaus Kellar", was so successful that it sold out days in advance, then General Manager Peter Gautschi's inspired proposal for a traditional Swiss restaurant was quickly approved by the board. Chesa, which means "house" or "inn" in the Romansch dialect, opened in August 1965. That year, Mr. Gautschi spent much of his vacation in the company of Dexter Yeh, whose firm, Dexon Ltd., was responsible for the restaurant's interior design. Together, they scoured Swiss villages and antique shops in search of authentic ornaments for the new venue. They had little trouble finding the roughly-hewn poppy seed grinder and the one-hand perpetual motion clock and they had their pick of old pewter spoons. The painted chest, probably made by a farmer in 1723, was a bit of a treasure. But Mr. Gautschi had his heart set on buying one of the old round wooden casks which people used to use for carrying wine with them into the mountains and these proved maddeningly elusive. Until one day, while dining in Zurich, he mentioned his quest to the restaurant owner, who, as it happened,

Mrs. Mao Keen Ying is a frequent visitor to this tiny pocket of Switzerland

had several of the old containers stored in her basement. Within a matter of days, two of the casks were dusted off, packed up and on the way to Hong Kong, where they still sit on a shelf in Chesa.

Chesa may do a roaring business ministering to homesick Swiss, but, even more importantly, it gained an early following in the local Hong Kong Chinese population, quelling worries about a supposed dislike of dairy products which might be assumed to bode ill for a fondue restaurant.

The Peninsula's wine cellars are home to a fine collection of vintage wines

Custom is evenly balanced between locals and foreigners.

If Chesa has set its own much-praised standard of friendly accommodation, the guests have responded in kind. Weekends and public holidays, the restaurant resounds with lively conversation, punctuated by laughter, as tables of regular customers settle in for an evening "at home". "Some guests have come every Sunday for 20 years," said restaurant manager Lam Siu Ping, "and many of our staff have been here for some 15 years, so our guests become friends." On one wall is painted a saying in Swiss-German which translates as: "A juicy sausage and a glass of Deltiner wine — not even a pretty girl can keep me from this." The chauvinism of the phrase might cause mild umbrage, but no Chesa regular would argue with the sentiment.

⚊◆◆▶

In The Peninsula's wine cellars (there are several), stored amongst the racks of Chateau Margaux, three-litre jeroboams of Bollinger, 1955 Sauternes, Chateau d'Yquem and the rare Montrachet 1988, are eight wines dating from the 1928 opening. The fragile labels bear the names Château Mouton-Rothschild, Château Cos D'Estournel, Château Haut-Brion and Château Beychevelle, among others. Along one wall of a climate-controlled room are rows of Cuvée Speciale Tattinger, specially bottled for the hotel's 50th anniversary, adorned by a picture of The Pen.

The faded labels of these rare vintages are mute reminders of those bygone summer revellers who ignored stultifying heat with glorious disregard; the wedding parties where hundreds of couples swept through the Ballroom; the arcane traditions that mystified the waiters at the St. Andrew's Society and St. George's balls; the pre-war optimists who danced at the last ball of the British Empire. The rich fabric woven over generations of refined, inspired entertaining forms a singular part of

The Bar has all the ingredients for a convivial evening

The Peninsula. But only a part — strolling through the hotel corridors, late on a Saturday evening, is an evocative experience. From high atop the tower, where a clutch of Cantonese movie stars makes a fashionably late entrance at Felix, to the party of old friends hovering pleasurably over Gaddi's luxurious cigar box, from the low bursts of laughter and song in The Bar to the final brandies being poured in Chesa, The Pen hums with sociability. The Grand Old Lady of Hong Kong is, indeed, dancing faster than ever.

THE PENINSULA AROUND THE WORLD

Over years of telling, the story has been lovingly buffed and burnished, with some bits perhaps so altered that, even if the protagonists could be identified, they might have trouble recognising themselves. The location, however, is undisputed: The Peninsula, Hong Kong, sometime during the early 1960s. A contemporary version of the tale describes a weary guest returning to his room after a lengthy, and, judging by the number of boxes and bags in the page boy's arms, triumphant shopping expedition. The gentleman's room attendant quickly arrived to assist with the careful hanging up of bespoke suits, monogrammed shirts and other accoutrements of elegant dressing. Finally, the attendant reached the last box. It held a pair of shoes. Holding them carefully on the palm of one hand, the room attendant inquired, "And would Sir like his shoes walked?"

Left, true dedication to service and comfort is the common thread linking every Peninsula hotel

Creative flourishes aside (in one version, the footwear is made of alligator skin), the essence of the tale, and its enduring popularity, illustrate the very heart and soul of Peninsula tradition, where a thoroughness of service is balanced with genuine warmth. When one travels to Peninsula hotels around the world, that dedication is a singular element, linking all the properties in an ambience that says "Peninsula" more eloquently than a logo or sign ever could.

Some traditions which have long been a feature of The Pen in Hong Kong have been welcomed in some of its sister hotels. Traditional English afternoon tea, for instance, has legions of fans beyond Hong Kong. Scones, *petit-fours* and pots of Darjeeling, Earl Grey and English Breakfast tea are served every afternoon in the Drawing Room of The Peninsula Beverly Hills, in the Gotham Lounge of The Peninsula

New York and in the Conservatory of The Peninsula Manila. Interestingly, Manila's social élite have echoed those habitués of the original Pen who view the east and west sides of the Lobby as distinct and separate territories. In The Peninsula Manila, sitting on the right side of the Lobby signals that you have "arrived", while those on the left are "aspiring to arrive". Whether founded in fact or fancy, the story lends a certain piquancy to people-watching in what has become the gathering spot for the rich and famous of Manila.

And yet "Peninsula" is not an imprint to be summarily stamped on each property bearing the name. Rather, it is an approach, an attitude. From Beijing to Beverly Hills, each hotel imparts its own distinctive ambience, with characteristics unique to its setting. The most obvious reflection of this is the use of art and architecture which reflect the culture of the surroundings. Philippine artist Napoleon Abueva's Sunburst sculpture dominates the stunning neo-classical lobby of The Peninsula Manila to magnificent effect. In New York, Hongkong and Shanghai Hotels, Limited's sympathetic renovation of a glorious structure in the heart of Manhattan that had for some years languished, empty and neglected, returned one of the most striking examples of Beaux Arts architecture to prominence. The preservation of the original sweeping staircases and fine exterior stonework enhances The Peninsula New York's sense of old world elegance and prestige.

Set amongst the pomp and circumstance of Hollywood, The Peninsula Beverly Hills eschews ostentation in favour of discreet comfort designed to make guests feel at home. Lush gardens, villas with separate entrances and poolside cabanas mean there's no shortage of the ultimate local luxury — privacy. In a lovely evocation of the Californian hotel's connection to the Orient, lacquer boxes are placed in the guest rooms. In Beijing, the drama and grace of traditional Chinese architecture are embodied in the striking red-tiled roof of The Palace Hotel, Beijing, located a short walk from the grandeur of the Forbidden City. Setting a new landmark on the banks of the Chao Phraya River, The Peninsula Bangkok pays homage to the rich tapestry of Thai culture through its artworks, furnishings and fabrics; The Peninsula Jakarta will follow suit in its own, very individual way.

As much a part of every Peninsula as the charm and elegance of style is the cutting-edge technology that reposes inside desk drawers, on bedside tables and behind wall panels. In every Peninsula property, the technology has been thoughtfully and capably designed for simplicity and flexibility. The Kowloon Hotel in Hong Kong is renowned as one of the world's most technologically advanced, and features in-room facsimile machines, electronic mail access whether guests are travelling with their personal computer or not and a Telecentre which provides computerised business and leisure information, message service and bill updates. The intensity of Hollywood's business environment is perfectly accommodated in The Peninsula Beverly Hills, where staff attending to poolside diners first take orders for telephones and fax machines, then tend to food and drink preferences.

Guests, too, contribute an essential defining factor. The Peninsula Hong Kong has welcomed generations of families, and they, in turn, have explored Peninsulas around the world as they travel for business and leisure, finding comfort in the assurance of The Peninsula standard. This assurance is enhanced by the presence of long-staying staff at each property and the group's overseas training programme, which promotes an awareness of other hotels, locales and people and contributes to the staff's breadth of experience.

Tradition, taste and assured service are Peninsula's building blocks around the world. Each property shapes this foundation with its own inimitable style and personality. Just as The Peninsula Hong Kong has bridged magnificently the graciousness of the past and a visionary concept of the future, so the group of hotels that shares its name draws on that legacy, building their future with character and style.

AFTERWORD

There's a spot in the boardroom where, by testing for slight variances in the "give" of the floor, you can stand balanced between the new tower and the original building; with one foot in the past, the other in the future. Above, in the foyer outside the function rooms, the join is more evident, if you're either a construction buff or have had it pointed out, that is. A polished brass plate, about 30 centimetres wide, travels along the floor, crossing doorways and expanses of carpet, covering the brief gap that exists between the hotel of the 1920s and the tower of the 1990s. The two structures have separate foundations; in strong winds, they move independently. And yet they are united in purpose and in origin.

Almost 70 years after the opening of The Peninsula ushered in a new era of luxury and comfort, the Grand Old Lady of Hong Kong is once again cloaked in the finery deserving of a legend. No silent witness, she has held court throughout Hong Kong's struggles and successes, its setbacks and achievements. During the arduous, frequently exhilarating journey from colonial backwater to economic powerhouse The Pen was both participant in and mirror of the times; a beautiful barometer forever monitoring the pulse of a vibrant city.

The Pen has always displayed a talent for nimbly crossing the tightrope of nostalgia and tradition on the one side, and vision and forward thinking on the other. "This company has shown a rare dedication to quality, and through the years, its executives, management team and staff have translated this into a distinctive philosophy," says Managing Director and Chief Executive Officer Pierre Boppe. "From this foundation comes an assurance which allows us to apply the lessons and successes

Left, The Peninsula staff's dedication to service is legendary

of the past in creating and interpreting a dynamic vision for the future."

It takes more than an elegant façade and tasteful decor to inspire the loyalty and affection that people feel for The Peninsula. The reassurance of the hotel's continual presence is an important factor, as is the constant upgrade of its services and facilities. But it is the people who are the heart and soul of The Pen, and it is they who infuse the hotel with a generous spirit and pride. "Whenever we come back, they say 'Welcome home'," said one long-time guest. "And they mean it." In the words of a former staff member, "The Peninsula reaches out, grabs hold of you and hugs you." Rare comfort, indeed.

THE PENINSULA HONG KONG — GENERAL MANAGERS

A.G. Piovanelli	1928 – 1940*	Felix Bieger	1980 – 1981
Aubrey Diamond	1940 – 1948*	Urs Aeby	1981 – 1986
Leo Gaddi	1948 – 1960	Eric Waldburger	1986 – 1990
Peter Gautschi	1960 – 1970	Felix Bieger	1990 – 1994
Felix Bieger	1970 – 1977	Peter Borer	1994 – present
Max Keller	1977 – 1980	*dates approximate, due to loss of records*	

INDEX